ESSAYS ON ENGLISH

ESSAYS ON ENGLISH

BY
BRANDER MATTHEWS

Essay Index Reprint Series

Originally published by
CHARLES SCRIBNER'S SONS
New York

 BOOKS FOR LIBRARIES PRESS
FREEPORT, NEW YORK

INTERNATIONAL STANDARD BOOK NUMBER:
0-8369-2285-9

LIBRARY OF CONGRESS CATALOG CARD NUMBER:
73-156693

PRINTED IN THE UNITED STATES OF AMERICA

To
OTTO JESPERSEN

CONTENTS

PAGE

I *Is the English Language Degenerating?*   1

II *What is Pure English?*   31

III *American English and British English*   59

IV *The Vicissitudes of the Vocabulary* .   79

V *The Latest Novelties in Language* . .   97

VI *Newspaper English*   119

VII *The Permanent Utility of Dialect* . .   137

VIII *A Confusion of Tongues*   155

IX *Learning a Language*   167

X *The Advertizer's Artful Aid* . . .   187

XI *A Standard of Spoken English* . .   205

XII *Style from Several Angles*   223

XIII *Mark Twain and the Art of Writing*   241

XIV *One World-Language or Two?* . . .   269

I

IS THE ENGLISH LANGUAGE
DEGENERATING?

I

IS THE ENGLISH LANGUAGE DEGENERATING?

I

THE American Academy of Arts and Letters accepted in 1917 a fund for the purpose of enabling it "to consider its duty towards the conservation of the English language in its beauty and purity"; and the Academy held several meetings to discover what its duty might be. At these meetings it was made evident that many, if not most, of those present were of opinion that the condition of our noble tongue was alarming and that this condition was perhaps even more alarming in the United States than it was in Great Britain.

One of those who contributed to the discussion went so far as to suggest that English as spoken and as written here in the United States had entered on a period of degeneracy not unlike that which befel Greek in the days of its decadence in what is known as the Hellenistic era. He cited the dictionary definition of "Hellenistic" as "resembling or partaking of

3

Greek character but not truly Hellenic" and as "combining Greek and foreign characteristics or elements." He ascribed the Hellenistic degradation of Greek to two causes. "In the first place, the change took place when the language was no longer young, with powers of expansion natural to youth, but was already mature and fixt . . . and in the second place, the change came when the language was no longer in the possession of the people alone who had created it, but was spoken and written over a vast territory among many peoples separated from the main stem by political and other traditions." He asserted that "neither one of these conditions singly would have produced quite the actual result, which was dependent on the conjunction of the two." He noted that these two conditions are conjoined here in the United States today, since English, "hardened by long usage," is "spread over a large territory among diverse peoples." And he feared that we could not escape the ugly conclusion that English has "entered upon a similar period" of disintegration.

This is an interesting suggestion; it seems to be supported by not a little evidence; it provides an easy explanation for the lapses from good usage obvious to all of us; it is persuasively plausible. But it will not resist scrutiny.

4

Fortunately for us, the alluring parallel is not borne out by the facts. The decline of Greek into Hellenistic laxity was not caused solely or even mainly by its "hardening" and by its "spreading over a wide territory." The debasing of Greek literature and the deterioration of the Greek language were due directly to the degeneracy of the peoples who spoke Greek. They had lost character as well as ability. They had become weaklings mentally and morally; the virtue had gone out of them; and as an inevitable consequence it had gone also out of the literature and out of the language. If the Greeks had kept their virility Greek would never have "hardened." So long as a people retains its vigor and its vital energy, its language never grows old; it preserves its health and its freshness; it has the secret of eternal youth. It will never suffer from creeping paralysis of style or from fatty degeneration of the vocabulary.

There is encouragement in recalling the fact that a language has no independent existence. Its strength depends upon the strength of those who speak it. Its extension is never due to its own merits, but always to the enterprise and the prowess of those who created it in their own image. "No speech can do more than express the ideas of those who employ it at the time,"

5

so Lounsbury assured us; and if these ideas are few and feeble the language also will become enfeebled. So long as the people is sturdy and resolute, so long as it holds its own in the rivalry of the nations, its language will be the fit instrument of its will. Linguistic decay is inseparable from racial decadence. Until the citizens of the United States and the inhabitants of the British Empire have lost both character and ability there is no danger that English will enter upon a period of Hellenistic disorganization, no matter how abundant and how diverse may be the superficial appearances which seem to point that way. So long as we are fit to do our share of the work of the world, we need not fear that our language will fail us in the hour of need.

II

THE suggestion was also made that the Hellenistic stage of a language "is in its very nature a paradox; it imports the union, or coexistence, of two hostile principles, unity and diversity, authority and independence, stability and mutation, tradition and ignorance." But this is not peculiar to a Hellenistic stage; it is a perennial paradox of human speech. At every moment of its existence every language is subject to these two hostile principles, authority

6

and independence, stability and mutation; and in fact it is by the interplay of these two opposing forces that the language is enabled to keep itself abreast of its work and to discharge the duties that are imposed upon it. Only when a language is dead or dying does it surrender itself to a blind obedience to tradition. So long as it is proud of its privileges as a living speech it dares diversity of usage and variety of vocabulary; and it ventures upon experiments often prompted by ignorance and sometimes none the less successful.

Despite the exacerbated protests of the upholders of authority and tradition a living language makes new words as these may be needed; it bestows novel meanings upon old words; it borrows words from foreign tongues; it modifies its usages to gain directness and to achieve speed. Often these novelties are abhorrent; yet they may win acceptance if they approve themselves to the majority. This irrepressible conflict between stability and mutation and between authority and independence can be observed at all epochs in the evolution of all languages, in Greek and in Latin in the past as well as in English and in French in the present. The man in the street is likely to have a relish for verbal novelty and even for verbal eccentricity; and the man in the library is likely to be a

7

stanch upholder of the good old ways, especially
hostile to what he contemptuously stigmatizes
as "neologisms," an abhorrent and horrific term
of reproach. Théophile Gautier, for example,
apparently regarded the French language in the
light of an exclusive club into which a new word
could be admitted only after being duly proposed and seconded and finally favorably reported by a committee on nominations. Swift
was vehement and vociferous in his demand for
power to forbid all innovation and to "fix" the
language once for all. Ben Jonson was objur-
gated by his rivals because he had put into circulation words of his own coinage; and yet he
once took occasion to declare that he loved
"pure and neat language . . . yet plaine and
customary."

The belief that a language ought to be "fixt,"
that is, made stable, or in other words, forbid-
den to modify itself in any way, was held by a
host of scholars in the seventeenth and eighteenth centuries. They were more familiar with
the dead languages, in which the vocabulary is
closed and in which usage is petrified, than they
were with the living languages, in which there
is always incessant differentiation and unending
extension. To "fix" a living language finally is
an idle dream; and if could be brought about it
would be a dire calamity. Luckily language is

never in the exclusive control of scholars; it does not belong to them alone, as they are often inclined to believe; it belongs to all who have it as a mother-tongue. It is governed not by elected representatives but by a direct democracy, by the people as a whole assembled in town-meeting. The younger and more active citizens of this linguistic community may propose new usages and new words and new meanings for old words; and the elder and more conservative citizens may protest against these novelties with all the weight due to seniority. And when both sides have been heard, there is a show of hands; and by this the irrevocable decision of the community itself is rendered.

When the community finds itself at a standstill because it lacks new words to name new things, it has to supply itself in a hurry. It makes the new word it needs when it feels the need; it has no time to submit the extemporized term to revision by a committee of scholars. The new word may be made in the library or in the laboratory, in the shop or in the street; it may be well made or ill made; but if it approves itself to the special group which needs it, it is likely at last to win acceptance from the rest of us. We Americans devised a new thing when we first built a huge receptacle for grain; and the men who devised this called it an *elevator*, which

9

does not seem to be the best possible name for that particular thing, but which is its name, none the less, and its only name. Almost at the same time, a word was needed for another novel device, that by which passengers could be carried to the upper floors of a building. The French termed this device an *ascender* (*ascenseur*); the Americans called it an *elevator*, in spite of the fact that they had just given the same name to another and wholly different instrument of advancing civilization; and the British preferred *lift*, perhaps the best of the three as the shortest and simplest.

Very often the verbal novelty is borrowed from a foreign tongue. "The great metropolitan English speech," so Emerson reminded us, is "the sea which receives tributaries from every region under Heaven." This is no merely modern activity, even if it may seem to be more frequent in the twentieth century than it was in the eighteenth. English began to appropriate words from other languages when it was in the early stage that we call Anglo-Saxon. This borrowing is wholly without danger to the purity of English if the word is definitely anglicized, if it is actually made to feel at home in our vocabulary, if it drops its alien accents and if it modifies its foreign pronunciation to adjust itself to our speech-habits. On the other hand, it must be regarded as a menace if it refuses to make this adjustment or if it cannot. So long as its users are conscious that it is foreign, so long as speakers try to give it its original pronunciation and so long as writers feel that they ought to indicate its exoticism by the use of italics, then it is a defilement of our native speech, since the foreign word discloses itself as a foreign substance merely imbedded in English and not really assimilated.

The new words, home-made or imported, may have been due to the effort of ignorance or they may have been inspired by tradition; they may be the result of individual independence or they may be sanctified by authority; they may win immediate acceptance or they may arouse prolonged controversy; but in the end they either fall out of use and into disrepute or they establish themselves in standard English. The ultimate decision as to their fate lies in the hands not of the educated alone or of the ignorant alone but of the main body of the users of English. When this verdict of the majority is once rendered, there is no appeal to a higher court. The decision stands for all time; and later generations will employ the verbal novelty unhesitatingly, ignorant that its validity had ever been a matter of dispute. Vaugelas, who helped to guide French in the right path, once put the case

II

in a nutshell: "There is only one master of language, who is the king and tyrant; this is usage."

III

OF the two causes to which were attributed the decline of the Greek language in its Hellenistic stage, one, its "hardening" because it was senile, has no parallel in the present condition of English. Our language is still capable of renewing its youth since the peoples who speak it have not lost their virility and their vivacity. But the other cause, the dispersion of the language "over a vast territory among many peoples separated from the main stem by political and other traditions"—this has its parallel in the present condition of English. We all know that our language is now "no longer in the possession of the people alone who created it." Indeed, English today occupies a position never before attained by any other tongue, in that it is the native speech of two great nations, politically distinct and more than once politically hostile to one another, the younger having now twice the population of the elder and the elder having become the center of a vast empire scattered on all the shores of all the seven seas. When Greek sank into its Hellenistic decay, Greece itself, and all the other places where

12

Greek was spoken, were ruled by alien Rome; and when Latin spread abroad, all those who spoke it were proud of their citizenship in the politically united empire which had brought peace to the world.

It may very well be asked if the condition which helped to bring about the degeneracy of Greek is not similar to that of English today, and if there is not a danger to the future of our language in its unprecedented dispersion and in its immediate contact with a host of other and inferior tongues. Not a few of those who have considered the consequences of this condition find it disquieting and doubt whether the substantial unity of English can be preserved much longer. They perceive an immediate menace in the abundance of Americanisms in the United States and in the prevalence of Briticisms in the little island where the language came to consciousness of its destiny. They fear that English may be split apart at last and separated into two rival tongues, American and British, with the breach between them steadily widening until they are as independent of one another as Spanish and Portuguese.

There is no denying that many facts might be adduced to justify this dread. There are indisputable differences between Londoner and New Yorker, in matters of cadence and of pronunciation, of vocabulary and of usage. An American straying near the Seven Dials feels himself as little at home linguistically as an Englishman wandering in the Five Points. A Boston man needs a glossary to enable him to interpret the jests of the cockney humorist; and an Oxford man might lay down Mr. Ade's 'Fables in Slang' in blank despair at his total inability to comprehend.

Yet when all is said the differences between British English and American English, however many they may be, are relatively few. The immense majority of words pass current on both sides of the Western Ocean. Many Americans do not find 'Fables in Slang' always easy to interpret; and no doubt there are recondite recesses of the cockney dialect that many Englishmen have never explored. Mark Twain might boast that he could speak the American language if he chose; but he did not choose, and his descriptions of the Sphinx and of the Jungfrau are written in English of a purity and a beauty unsurpassed in the pages of any contemporary British author. The divergencies of speech between the United States and Great Britain are not important and are not more marked than those between two sections in the same country, between Yorkshire and Wessex for example, or between Boston and Wyoming.

If Mark Twain might be summoned again as a witness, he would testify to the linguistic gulf which yawned between Scotty Briggs and the minister who was requested to officiate at Buck Fanshaw's funeral;—and yet both of them were native Americans. Probably an equal gap would divide a Cambridge don and a Cornish miner.

Separatist tendencies are ever at work in every language; and they are constantly overcome by the cohesive restraint of a common literature. The centrifugal force of geographic dispersion is conquered by the centripetal force of a standard language chosen out of current speech, carefully selected, recognized as a standard, imposed by the school-teacher and spread abroad by the printing press. The Hellenistic decay of Greek was due mainly to the degeneracy of the Greeks themselves; but it might have been arrested, more or less, if a knowledge of standard Greek had been carried by books and magazines and newspapers to all those who spoke the language and if there had been schools everywhere impressing upon the young the nobility of the tongue in which Homer had told the early legends of the race. It is quite possible that if printing had been invented and if schools had been set up in the Iberian peninsula before the differentiation of Portuguese and

Spanish, those two languages might not have gone each on its own way and we might have had a single Iberian speech strengthened by the best elements of both the existing tongues.

Localisms, — Briticisms and Americanisms, Australianisms and Afrikanderisms—may be frequent in the casual conversation of the street and of the shop; but they have not affected and they are not likely to affect the standard English of books and of school-books. Localisms appear in print only rarely; and mainly in the dialog of fiction. In British novels we have a parade of Scotticisms and of Hibernicisms, just as in American short-stories we have the vernacular of the Yankee and the picturesque vocabulary of the Westerner. But these works of fiction aiming at local color and local flavor confine the localisms to the dialog; and the narrative passages are written in scholarly fashion. Sir James Barrie is not more careful in his style than Joel Chandler Harris; and Rudyard Kipling is not more conscientious than Bret Harte. The American writers eschew overt Americanisms as rigorously as the British writers strive to avoid Briticisms. Slang and its analogs—the contorted vocables of the Babu, for instance—are to be found chiefly in a few writings of the professed humorists, such as George Ade and "F. Anstey." It is obvious that the 'Courting'

of Lowell and the 'Tam o' Shanter' of Burns are
not more threatening to the purity of English
than the Welsh and the Irish which Shakspere
put into the mouths of two of the characters
who fellowship with Falstaff.

IV

A STUDENT of the evolution of English may
even be emboldened to go further and to declare
that there is not only no peril to our language
in the wide dispersion of those who speak it,
but to assert that there may even be actual
advantage as a result of this geographic and
racial diversity. English altho old is ever
young; it has matured, but it has not hardened;
it is continually replenishing its store. Like
the two great nations who have it as their
mother-tongue, it is forever increasing its population and rectifying its frontiers. It needs new
words and it admits them to citizenship only
after they have been tried and tested. Now,
as these two nations spread themselves they
come into contact with strange peoples and they
annex words from the several tongues of these
outlanders to the constant enrichment of English. Words—good words and true—are taken
over from the American Indian and from the Indian of Hindustan, from the Malay, the Eskimo,

17

and the islander of the South Seas. And the self-governing dominions of the British Commonwealth and the semi-independent states of the American Union are all of them proving-grounds for verbal seedlings which may in time be transplanted and acclimated in standard English.

This is in accord with the immemorial custom of the language. English has always been in the habit of amplifying its vocabulary since the distant time hundreds of years ago when it was only one of half-a-dozen rival dialects in use among the descendants of the Angles and the Saxons. When we go back to consider the origins of the modern languages we find that they are the results of a series of happy accidents. In the earlier Middle Ages no nation had any consciousness of its racial unity; in fact, there were no nations (in any modern sense of the word), and therefore no national languages. There was local loyalty to the town, and possibly even to the province, of which the town was the center; and one local dialect was as good as another. Italian is today what it is only because Dante made use of his native Tuscan as the tongue in which to paint his mighty vision of the universe; and if he had been a Neapolitan, a *cent* would not now be a *soldo*, it would be a *sordo*. French is what it is because

the rulers of Paris extended their sway generation after generation over Brittany and Nor-
mandy, Burgundy and Gascony, Alsace and
Provence, thereby establishing the predomi-
nance of the dialect of the Isle de France, even
over Provençal which had earlier possest a
flourishing literature of its own. If the rulers
of Provence had had a superior ambition, wiser
statesmanship, and more aggressive prowess,
yes would not now be *oui*, it would be *oc*.

So English is what it is because England
unified itself early with London as its capital
and because Chaucer used the East-Midland
dialect as the medium in which to dramatize his
human comedy. In itself the dialect of London
was not superior to that of York or of Bath, just
as the dialect of Florence was not superior to
that of Naples or the dialect of Paris to that of
Avignon. But once established as the vehicle
of literature, the dialects of London, of Florence,
and of Paris drew largely and repeatedly upon
the linguistic resources of their former rivals
which sank inevitably into indisputable inferiority. Perhaps it is because Germany until
the eighth decade of the nineteenth century was
not united in a nation, conscious of its unity,
because Germany has not even yet a single
capital, that German is now linguistically the
most backward of the modern languages, the

one in which there is the widest gap between the standard speech of the stage and of literature and the ordinary usage of everyday life. To the rest of the world German is still an uncouth tongue, in which there are a host of books well worth reading and very hard to read.

The standard of English is now solidly establisht in its literature. It no longer depends on the local dialect of East-Midland in which it had its origin. We may go further and assert that it is no longer in the exclusive custody of the inhabitants of the island where it grew to maturity. Like every other tongue it belongs to all those who speak it, wherever they may have been born and wherever they may live, in Portland, England, in Portland, Maine, or in Portland, Oregon. Its future is conditioned by its past; and it is free to expand only in accord with the practice of those who have ennobled it by their mastery of its secrets. And as in the beginning, so now and to the end, it will go on strengthening itself and increasing its wealth by levying on the words and the phrases and the usages which approve themselves to one or another of the several communities who speak it and who write in it loyalty to their inheritance of its guardianship.

Thus we are led to the conclusion that the dispersion of those who speak English is not now a danger or even a disadvantage. We can see that there may even be advantage for standard English in that it can adopt, whenever it sees fit, the new words first tried out in one or another of its separate territories. These new words are at first only localisms, British or American or Australian. They may not survive for long; they may remain localisms doomed to perish sooner or later; or they may be adopted at last by the main body of those who speak English and who write it. *Cad* and *fad* were at first only localisms; they were Briticisms struggling for existence and getting slowly into sporadic use in England, until at last they achieved a peaceful penetration into the United States. Then they ceased to be mere Briticisms, because they won recognition as useful words worthy of admission into standard English. A like fate has befallen *boss* and *boom*, the first a localism of New York (descended from the days when the Empire City was New Amsterdam), and the second a spontaneous creation of the lumber-camps of Michigan. In time these two Americanisms were in common use all over the United States; and they were then merely Americanisms; yet after a while they made their way into the British Empire, until now both of them bid fair to be lifted into standard English.

Rough, a Briticism for *loafer*, is now in reputable use among all who write English; and perhaps a corresponding Americanism, *tough*, will also be promoted, to be followed in the course of time by the Australianism *larrikin* and the Californianism *hoodlum*. On the other hand there seems to be little likelihood that the Americanism *back of* (as a synonym for *behind*) will ever win favor in the British Isles or that the Briticism *directly* (for *as soon as*) will ever be accepted on our side of the Atlantic. There is of course no presumption in favor of a localism born in Great Britain any more than there is a presumption against one born in the United States or in Australia.

There is comfort for those who are fearful of of an impending contamination and corruption of English in Lounsbury's summing up of the situation as it appeared to him a quarter of a century ago. He asserted that English is now "the language of vast communities, and, through the operation of manifold agencies is daily growing in universality and power. The whole tremendous machinery of education is constantly at work to strengthen it, to broaden it, to bring it into conformity with the speech of the humblest as well as of the highest. Day by day dialectic differences disappear; day by day the standard tongue, in which is embodied

22

classical English literature, is widening and deepening its hold upon every class."

V

THE French are more fortunate than we who speak English in that the French Academy has been formally charged with supervision over the language. The statutes of its foundation, under the wise rule of the far-seeing Richelieu, asserted that "the Academy's principal function shall be to work with all the care and all the diligence possible at giving sure rules to our language, and rendering it pure, eloquent, and capable of treating the arts and sciences." In its two centuries and a half of honorable existence the French Academy has never forgotten this injunction, altho it has never worked "with all the diligence possible." Yet it did get out its dictionary at last; and it has brought out revisions of this dictionary from time to time, authorizing new words, new usages, new orthographies. Its decisions on these matters are treated with great respect; they are instantly accepted by all the schools in France; they supply that final standard to which most men are glad to conform. M. Henri Bergson, in an address before the American Academy of Arts and Letters in the spring of 1917, declared that the power of the French Academy over the French language is complete. He insisted that a word which is not French in the morning may be French in the evening,—if the Academy has held a meeting in the afternoon at which it was approved. This is an extreme statement of an extreme opinion as to the linguistic autocracy of the Academy. On board ship when the mate has taken the observation and reported that it is noon, the captain replies, "Make it so," whereupon eight bells are sounded; but at that moment in that longitude and in that latitude it would then be noon, even if the captain had not issued his confirmatory command.

It is a condition and not a theory which confronts us when we consider the relation of the French Academy to the French language. The theory may be as M. Bergson asserted; but the condition is that the speech of forty millions of men and women cannot be confided to the exclusive control of forty elderly gentlemen, however lofty their merits and however extended their learning. Moreover, every one of these elderly gentlemen is probably in the habit of using a host of words and phrases not yet sanctioned by his colleagues and by himself. Collectively the Academy may ignore the existence of these novel terms and usages; yet the individual Academician may have no doubt as to their utility and therefore their propriety.

24

In the final chapter of his history of the French language, M. Brunot asserted that "the French Academy is officially entrusted with the control of the French language; but itself aware that it is powerless to restrain the flood of verbal novelties, it makes no effort to do so. Declining the suggestion that it should itself remake ill-made words, it continues, in accord with its tradition, to register accepted usages, when the public has pronounced a verdict on them. It does not aspire to guide the public, but only to follow it. . . . And what authority can a body possess, the members of which as individuals, are incessantly violating the decisions of the court they belong to,—freeing themselves in their own writings from the rules they have shared in formulating?"

In his famous essay on the 'Literary Influence of Academies,' written more than half a century ago, Matthew Arnold held that the French Academy imposed a high standard in matters of taste. "To give the law, the tone to literature, and that tone a high one, is its business." And he credited to the existence of the Academy certain superiorities which he recognized in French literature. Arnold admitted that the French Academy itself owed "its existence to a national bent towards the things of the mind, towards culture, towards clearness, correctness and propriety in thinking and speaking." And his admission suggests a doubt as to whether the French Academy is not really a consequence rather than a cause of the culture of France, whether it is not merely an outward and visible sign of French characteristics. Nietzsche, for example, found in the French themselves three distinguishing qualities: a gift of form, a psychologic sensibility, a reunion of the special characteristics of the peoples of the north and of the peoples of the south. Surely these gifts would suffice to endow the language and the literature of France with the clarity and the culture which we discover in them.

Yet, whether it is a cause or a consequence, the French Academy amply justifies its existence. It is a tower of strength to the forces which make for authority and tradition, unity and stability. At the same time the culture, the intelligence and the urbanity, of its two score members chosen from every department of literature,—all these tend to preserve its open-mindedness and to prevent its assuming a permanent attitude of arbitrary hostility towards a new word simply because it is new.

VI

IF after three hundred years of authority consecrated by its charter, the venerable French Academy can do as little as it now dares to do, what can an American Academy of Arts and Letters, less than a score of years old, and having no official warrant, do for the purity and the beauty of the English language? The hasty answer to this question would be that it can do nothing. Even if this answer is found, on closer analysis, to be wrong, there is difficulty in declaring just what it can do, while there is no difficulty in declaring what it had better not do. For its own sake the American Academy had better refrain from assuming any attitude implying that it has any claim to dictate decisions. It lacks the long tradition and the official standing of its French predecessor; and the peoples who speak English are less regardful of authority, even when consecrated by the centuries, than the people who speak French. The suggestions of the American Academy can have only the weight due to the reputations of its several members; and it must exist for scores of years before its collective opinions—if it ever formulates any—can expect to be received with reverence.

For this reason, and for others also, we may

rest assured that the American Academy will not inflict upon the public any index of inacceptable words and of disreputable usages. Probably it would not be possible to get its members to agree upon any list of verbal taboos. The word which might seem to one perfectly acceptable would be to another the abomination of desolation; and the usage satisfactory to many might be anathema to a few. The educated, no less than the illiterate, are inclined to hold that the phrase to which they are accustomed is immitigably right. Every one of us is prone to erect a purely personal standard and to be impatiently intolerant of those who decline to bow down to it.

There are numberless conflicting usages, as to each of which each of us has his own preference; and in many cases there is nothing on which to base a final verdict. The appeal to precedent is tempting, but a living language refuses to be bound by its past. The present always insists on making its own precedents; and it always reserves the right to recall judicial decisions even if this may necessitate an amendment to the constitution. The dead hand is never allowed to throttle the living tongue. The only tribunal whose judgment is final is the next generation; and we shall not survive to see it attain to years of discretion.

28

The American Academy will be wise in refusing to promulgate any index expurgatorius, altho its individual members will be free to urge their own preferences. It will be wise also if it refrains from lending support to the efforts of pedants and pedagogs to cramp the freedom of the language by importing into English rules valid in other tongues but unwarranted in ours, and by imposing upon English other rules evolved out of their own inner consciousness. In most of our grammars, perhaps in all of those issued earlier than the opening of the twentieth century, we find linguistic laws laid down which are in blank contradiction with the genius of the language, and which seem to justify a pernicious insistence upon the alleged grammatical blunders to be discovered in the works of the masters of English.

What the American Academy can do for the preservation of the purity and the beauty of the English language, is to aid in arousing a livelier interest and to help in the dissemination of sounder knowledge. Information as to the essential principles of linguistic growth is not common property; and it is needed by the educated almost as much as by the uneducated. By addresses and by essays purity may be more clearly defined and beauty may be more justly estimated. False beliefs may be discredited and affectations may be exposed to scorn. Attention may be called to the waste of effort and to the ultimate futility which results from the attempt of eager and ardent youngsters to express themselves in disregard of the conquests of the past. It cannot be emphasized too often or too strenuously that for this generation progress is possible, not by starting anew from the beginning, but only by going on from the point attained by the older generations.

By an appeal to the public, direct and incessant, by word of mouth and by the printed page, the members of the American Academy can insist on the value of our linguistic inheritance, on our possession of a language incomparably simple in its grammar and incomparably comprehensive in its vocabulary. They can remind us Americans, descended from many stocks and united with the British by law and literature and language, of the preciousness of our English speech, the mother-tongue of two mighty nations, inherited by us from our grandfathers and by us to be handed down to our grandchildren, unimpaired in vigor and in variety, in freshness and in nobility. More than that it will not be wise for the American Academy to attempt.

(1918.)

II

WHAT IS PURE ENGLISH?

II

WHAT IS PURE ENGLISH?

I

THERE is no topic about which men dispute more frequently, more bitterly, or more ignorantly than about the right and the wrong use of words. Even political questions and religious questions can be debated with less acrimony than linguistic questions. The usual explanation of this unexampled acerbity in discussion is probably accurate; it is that our political and our religious opinions are our own and we are individually responsible for them, whereas our linguistic opinions are the result of habits acquired from those who brought us up, so that aspersions on our parts of speech appear to us to be reflections on our parents. To misuse words, to make grammatical blunders is an evidence of illiteracy; and to accuse a man of illiteracy is to disparage the social standing of his father and his mother.

The uneducated are inclined to resent any speech more polished than their own; and the half-educated are prompt to believe that their

33

half-knowledge includes all wisdom. As the half-educated acquired their half-knowledge from a teacher who relied on some work, grammar or dictionary, they naturally turn to a book of one of these two kinds as to an inspired oracle, accepting what they find therein as indisputable. They do not suspect that the immense majority of the grammars which were in use in our schools until very recently abounded in unfounded assertions about our language and laid down rules without validity. And one immediate result of this has been singularly unfortunate. Since some of these newfangled regulations had not been known to the translators of the Bible, to Shakspere and to Milton, students were called upon to point out the so-called errors in the writings of these mighty masters of language! Not only was this absurd, it was also injurious in that it misdirected the effort of those who wished to learn how to use English accurately. It focused attention on the purely negative merit of avoiding error instead of centering it on the positive merit of achieving sincerity, clarity, and vigor. The energies of the students were wasted, and worse than wasted, in the futilities of "linguistic manicuring"—as President Stanley Hall once contemptuously termed it.

The same attitude had been taken by the

34

highly trained Roman rhetoricians towards certain of the Fathers of the Church, the vernacular vigor of whose writing did not please the ultra-refined ears of the overeducated critics. After recording this fact in his study of the 'End of Paganism,' the wise and urbane Gaston Boissier remarked that "when we have spent all our lives recommending purity and correctness and elegance, that is to say, the lesser merits of style, we often become incapable of seeing its larger merits"; and "we set up a standard of perfection, based rather on the absence of defects than on the presence of real qualities; and we are no longer apt to appreciate what is new and original." The refined taste of the overeducated is always likely to be more appreciative of the absence of defects than of the presence of what is new and original.

Like the Roman rhetoricians contemporary with Tertullian our linguistic manicurists are forever recommending purity and correctness and elegance, three qualities not easy to define,—or rather to be defined by every one of us in accord with his own personal equation. Elegance is a quality to be attained only by those who do not stoop to seek it too assiduously. Correctness is likely to be interpreted as a compliance with the rules as laid down by the uninspired grammarians rather than an

35

obedience to the larger laws whereby the language is freely guided. And purity,—that is a chameleon word, if ever there was one; it changes meaning while we are looking at it.

II

In all probability most of those who are insisting upon the preservation of the purity of our language mean that English must be kept free from contamination by foreign tongues, that we who use it must refrain from borrowing words from other languages, and from making new words of our own, and that, in short, we must stick to the old stock and use nothing but what an impassioned orator once called "real Angular-Saxon." Now, it needs but a moment's reflection to show that an insistence on this kind of purity would be most unfortunate, since it would hamper the necessary development of the language and since it would prevent English from exercising its immemorial privilege of helping itself to all sorts of terms from all sorts of languages, ancient and modern. To the exercise of this indisputable right English owes its unparalleled richness of vocabulary and its unequaled wealth of words more or less equivalent yet deftly discriminated by delicate shades of difference.

36

Of course, this power to enrich itself from other tongues is not peculiar to English; and every other language has profitably availed itself of the same privilege. When Latin was a living speech it was continually levying upon Greek for the terms it lacked itself. In Latin the vocabulary of philosophy, for example, was almost exclusively derived from the Greek, just as in English the vocabularies of war, of millinery, and of cookery are derived from the French. And even in Cicero's time there were not wanting purists among the Latins who protested against these foreign importations, and who besought their fellow-Romans to be satisfied with native words of the good old Italic stock.

The attitude of these Latin purists was precisely that of the German Emperor when he requested his subjects to be as Teutonic as possible in their speech, and to abandon the use of French terms on their bills-of-fare, translating the names of all dishes into German, and renouncing the traditional Gallic terminology of the dinner-table. Oddly enough, he did not propose to de-gallicize the terminology of the parade-ground, and to prescribe Teutonic equivalents for *lieutenant*, *captain*, *colonel*, and *general*. But he did go so far as to suggest the rejection of *telephone* in favor of a word "made in Ger-

37

many," *fern-sprecher*, "far-speaker." Perhaps he did not know that the name of the useful American implement is not French in its origin, but German, devised by Reis for his instrument to transmit sounds (altho it could not convey articulate speech). The Kaiser's motive was understandable, but none the less was his action unfortunate, since the result of the acceptance of his advice would be to deny to his people the use of a name internationally accepted. Here patriotic bias seems to have misled the German Emperor as it had earlier misled the Iron Chancellor. Bismarck strenuously opposed the sensible movement for the more general employment of the Roman letters used by nearly all other countries, urging the retention of the ugly and awkward German text-letter, a medieval alphabet surviving only in the Teutonic countries, altho it is not in any way specifically Teutonic.

There is however one native German addition to the Teutonic military vocabulary,— *Kriegs-Herr*, which strictly speaking means merely *Commander-in-Chief* but which has lent itself to a mistranslation into *War-Lord*, thereby seeming to suggest unhappy implications. The Kaiser was no more a War-Lord in the sinister sense of the term than is the President of the United States, who is also constitutionally

38

charged with the chief command of all our forces on land and sea. If the Germans had an international name for *Commander-in-Chief*, familiar to all peoples rather than a purely native name, *Kriegs-Herr*, there would have been no need for them to explain away a misunderstanding natural enough among those whose acquaintance with German permitted them to translate only syllable by syllable.

A certain number of modern scientific technical terms are the same in all the modern languages, because they were adopted by an authorized international conference, empowered to standardize these essential elements of scientific nomenclature. Not a few of this little group of nouns reveal at once the cosmopolitan courtesy which presided at their creation, since they are made from the names of the pioneers of investigation in the several countries where modern science has most rapidly advanced. The *volt* takes its name from an Italian, the *ohm* from a German, the *ampere* from a Frenchman, the *watt* and the *farad* from two Englishmen and the *henry* from an American. From these root words, each with its precise meaning, a host of compounds have been made, of which *voltage* and *kilo-watts* are the most familiar to the layman.

III

IF the preservation of the purity of English meant that we must follow the example of the German Emperor, and strive to exclude from our language every word not native to our speech, erecting a prohibitive tariff-wall to keep out all imported terms, then it would become the duty of every lover of our noble tongue to advocate the impurity of English. To do its work, our language, like every other, ancient and modern, needs now and again to be replenished and reinvigorated by fresh blood. Just as the population of the British Isles is Celtic and Roman, Anglo-Saxon and Norman, and just as the population of the United States is compounded of a variety of ethnic ingredients, so the English language, the joint-possession of British and Americans, is itself a melting-pot, a linguistic crucible into which have been thrown words from every possible source. A shrewd Englishman once declared, "we choose words, like servants, for their usefulness, and not for their pedigree."

As the vocabularies of war, of millinery, and of cookery have been recruited from the French, so the vocabulary of shipping has been recruited from the Dutch and the Scandinavian, and the vocabulary of music from the Italian. The vocabulary of philosophy is partly Latin but mainly Greek; and modern science draws freely on both of the classic tongues when it is forced to manufacture the manifold new terms it needs for its endless inventions and discoveries. Even the rude dialects of the American Indians have been laid under contribution to describe things native to North America—*moccasin*, for example, and *wigwam*, *tepee*, and *totem*. These words were imported into English because no domestic manufacturer had supplied anything as satisfactory. Purists may rage and precisians may imagine a vain thing; but this is what English will do in the future as it has done in the past. "No tongue can possibly be corrupted by alien words which convey ideas that cannot be expressed by native ones," said that open-minded and plain-spoken scholar, the late Professor Lounsbury. Elsewhere in his brilliant history of our language the same writer reassured those who confounded purism and purity. "Terminations and expressions which had their origin in ignorance and misapprehension are now accepted by all; and the employment of what was at first a blunder has often become subsequently a test of propriety of speech." So we may take heart of grace; we need not be downcast; what the language has done with profit in the years that have gone before, it may

WHAT IS PURE ENGLISH?

do with impunity in the years that are to come.

In all these cases the words which were adopted from foreign tongues are now regarded as native by the mass of those who use them with no knowledge of their exotic origin. They have been completely assimilated; and the language is the richer for their inclusion within it. Even the most pedantic of purists unconsciously employs countless terms which he would be compelled by his principles to reject if he stopped to consider that they are not outgrowths of the native stock. We all use words for what they mean to us now and here, without regard to their remoter source in some other tongue once upon a time and without regard to their exact meaning in that other tongue. "Language as written, as spoken is an art and not a science," so one of the least pedantic of American scholars has asserted; and then this veteran student of language, Professor Gildersleeve, added the encouraging comment that "the study of origins, of etymology has very little, if anything, to do with the practice of speaking and writing. The affinity of English with Greek and Latin is a matter that does not enter into the artistic consciousness of the masses that own the language."

To the pedants and to the purists no declaration could be more shocking than that the masses own the language; and yet no assertion is more solidly rooted in the fact, and more often emphasized by those who have trained themselves to a mastery of their own tongue. The fastidious French poet, Malherbe, when asked as to the propriety of a word, used to refer the inquirer to the porters of the Haymarket in Paris, saying that these were his masters in language. The fastidious Cicero was constantly refreshing his own scholarly vocabulary by the apt terms he took from Plautus, who had found them in the tenements of the Roman populace. And the wise Roger Ascham put the case pithily when he wrote in his 'Toxophilus' that "he that will write well in any tongue must follow the counsel of Aristotle, to speak as the common people do, to think as the wise men do."

IV

LANGUAGE can be made in the library no doubt, and in the laboratory also, but it is most often and most effectively created in the workshop and in the market-place, where the imaginative energy of our race expresses itself spontaneously in swiftly creating the lacking term in response to the unexpected demand. Nothing could be better, each in its way, than picturesque vocables like *scare-head* and *loan-*

shark, wind-jammer and *hen-minded,* all of them
casual American contributions to the English
language, and all of them examples of the
purest English. *Hen-minded* is an adjective
devised by Howells to describe the "women
who are so common in all walks of life, and who
are made up of only one aim at a time, and of
manifold anxieties at all times." *Scare-head*
and *loan-shark* are probably the products of the
newspaper office, always awake to the immediate utility of a vivid vocable. *Wind-jammer*
was put together by some down-east sailor-
man, inheritor of the word-forming gift of his
island ancestors who helped to harry the Ar-
mada. "*Wind-jammer,*" remarked Professor
Gildersleeve, trained by his intimate knowledge
of Greek to appreciate verbal vigor as well as
verbal delicacy, "*Wind-jammer* is a fine word,
I grant, and so is every Anglo-Saxon compound
that grows and is not made."

The words evolved in the work-shop and in
the street are likely to be less pretentious and
more picturesque than those put together in the
library and in the laboratory. Often they have
a vernacular vigor of their own, almost Elizabethan in its freshness. To the men of the
railroad we owe the verbs to *side-track* and to
side-swipe, sharply expressive and instantly understandable. They are the result of the util-

44

ization of the immemorial privilege of making a verb out of a noun, a privilege which is one of the most precious possessions of our English speech. Roosevelt recorded one occasion when he was present at the making of a new and superbly expressive verb in accord with this principle. When he was a ranchman he had aided two of his men in felling a group of trees; and he chanced to overhear one of these employees explain that "Bill cut down fifty-three, I cut forty-nine, and the boss he *beavered* down seventeen." With full appreciation of the point thus made against his skill, Roosevelt commented that "those who have seen the stump of a tree which has been gnawed down by a beaver will understand the exact force of the comparison."

To *side-track* and to *side-swipe* may be companioned by to *side-step*, probably due to the verbal inventiveness of an unliterary admirer of the manly art of self-defense. But where shall we class another and even more satisfactory term called into being by the wordmaking faculty of the man in the street? Who was it who first dared to employ the delectable adjective *pussy-footed?* Here is an American invention which would have filled Ben Jonson with joy, and which he would have taken over with glee. Our own men of letters are more timor-

45

ous, more traditional and less receptive. So it is that *pussy-footed* has not yet been welcomed into the dictionary, and a college president would probably hesitate to use it in a commencement address, even if he might employ it with relish in his ordinary conversation. And scarcely less expressive is the finely imagined noun *high-brow*, a lovely word to describe an unlovely creature. Perhaps neither of them would have found favor from Julius Cæsar, who laid down as a linguistic law that "one should avoid an unexampled word as one would a rock." Yet if the man who dared at last to cross the Rubicon had avoided all the rocks he found in his path, he would never have arrived at Rome, even if all the roads led there.

We may venture to believe that *wind-jammer* and *hen-minded*, *pussy-footed* and *high-brow* would have delighted Lowell; they meet the simple test that he laid down in one of his letters:—"A word that cleaves to the memory is always a good word—that's the way to test them." And we cannot doubt that Lowell would have relished another American creation, due to the humorous ingenuity of Mr. James L. Ford,—*culturine*, a most admirable word to describe the affectation of those who pretend to culture without having the education out of which only can true culture flower. These are all new

words, and they are all good words; but we must
not fail to remember that not all new words
are good words. Ben Jonson, who was himself
a frequent maker of new words, displayed his
shrewdness when he declared that "Custom is
the most certain Mistress of Language, as the
publicke stampe makes the current money,"
adding as a caution, "But wee must not be too
frequent with the mint, every day coyning."

V

OUR treasury is enriched when we take over
needed terms from abroad and re-issue them
stamped with our own image and superscrip-
tion. There is no danger to the purity of English if the borrowed words are absolutely assimilated; but there is damage when they remain
outlanders and refuse to take out their naturalization papers. *Moccasin* and *boss*, *lieutenant*
and *omelet*, *waltz* and *tremolo* are now citizens
of our vocabulary, altho they were once immigrants admitted on sufferance. Unfortunate-
ly, there is a host of other linguistic importations which have retained their foreign spelling, often with alien accents, and which have
kept their un-English pronunciation. *Ennui*
and *genre* and *nuance* are not yet acclimated in
English speech, because they cannot be pro-

nounced properly by those unfamiliar with spoken French. Quite as bad is the case of *défi* and *métier* and *rôle*, all of which still wear the accents of their native tongue, abhorrent in English orthography.

These friendly aliens have not yet been admitted to full citizenship in English, because they have not yet renounced their former allegiance to French. Altho the French themselves have welcomed fewer immigrants from English than English has from French, they are stricter than we are in insisting on imposing French costumes on the applicant for sanctuary. In Paris the wandering American may order a *redingote;* and the tailor who makes it for him will not know that the garment is the same as the English *riding-coat*. In Paris again the wandering Briton may enter a restaurant and ask for a *biftek* or for a slice of *rosbif*, just as in London a wondering Gaul can be served with a *fillet* of sole, altho the cockney waiter may never have heard that the English word began life as a French word, *filet*, slightly altered in its spelling and slightly modified in its pronunciation to conform to the laws of our own language.

In Russia, so we are told, the English word *shocking* has been acquired from the French who use it a little sarcastically to indicate the horrified reaction of the mid-Victorian British matron forced to behold what offends her delicate susceptibility as Gallic impropriety. Having appropriated the word, the Russians have made it their own, bestowing upon it all the variety of terminations to which it would be entitled if it had been native to the Russian tongue. And this is as it should be; and it is a good example for us to follow. If an imported word refuses to swear allegiance to the constitution of the English language and if it does not promise to obey our linguistic laws, it is an undesirable citizen of the vocabulary to be deported summarily and speedily. And there is a horde of alien words detained at the Ellis Island of the English language demanding admission and yet unwilling to accept the conditions of citizenship. There is the immediately obvious case of *camouflage*, for example, an exotic vocable as prevalent to-day as *fin de siècle* was a score of years ago. It is to be hoped that its vogue will be as evanescent as that of its predecessor, now sunk beneath the waters of oblivion.

Probably *chauffeur* and *garage*, *chassis* and *limousine* have come to stay; they are not transients but permanent boarders in that Inn of Strange Meetings which the English language is. But *chauffeur* and *chassis* offensively violate

the principles of English orthography; and
garage still preserves its foreign pronunciation
—altho there are some already who have had
the courage to speak it as tho it rimed with
carriage, thus anglicizing it once for all. It is
pleasant to see that there are others who do not
shrink from speaking and writing *risky* in place
of *risqué* and *brusk* in place of *brusque*, just as
the French have transmogrihed *beefsteak* into *biftek* and *roastbeef* into *rosbif*.

There is no reason why *garage* should not be
pronounced to rime with *carriage*, just as *charade*
now rimes with *aid*. Our kin across the sea
still give to the final syllable of *charade* its
original French sound, as they also preserve the
French pronunciation of *trait*, riming it to *stray*
whereas we Americans rime it to *straight*. The
British seem to be in doubt still whether *hotel* is
really an English word; and they write and
speak of *an* hotel, respecting the silent *h* of the
French. Perhaps it is due to the cockney trick
of dropping the *h* that the British say *an* hospital and that Mr. Rudyard Kipling entitled
one of his short-stories 'An Habitation Enforced.' Americans would no more write *an*
habitation than they would write *an* house or
an home.

The real danger of impurity lies not in our
taking over foreign terms, but in our employing

them without taking them over completely. Either a word is English or it is not. If it is not English, a speaker or a writer who knows his business ought to be able to get along without it. There is no imperative call for us to borrow *mise-en-scène* and *première*, for instance, *artiste* and *dénouement, zeitgeist* or *rifaciamento;* and it is perfectly possible to express in our own tongue the meanings conveyed by these terms, imported in the original package.

On the other hand if a word is now English, whatever its earlier origin, then it ought to be treated as English, deprived of its foreign accents and forced to take an English plural. No one doubts for a moment that *cherub* and *criterion, gymnasium* and *index* can claim good standing in our English vocabulary, yet we find a pedant now and then who still bestows upon these helpless words the plurals they had to use in their native tongues and who therefore writes *cherubim* and *criteria, gymnasia* and *indices*, violating the grammatical purity of English. The pedant who is guilty of this affectation is "showing off," as the boys say; he is displaying his acquaintance with foreign languages and he is thus revealing his ignorance of his own tongue. It is blank ignorance intensified by sheer affectation which tempts any one to speak of a *foyer*-hall or of a *grille*-room, misbegotten hybrids impossible to a man who is on speaking terms with either English or French. This same combination of ignorance and affectation is responsible for *employé* and *répertoire* when we have already the simple English *employee* and *repertory*. It may be suggested also that as we have long had *interrogatory*, we do not really need *questionnaire*, and that if we prefer to borrow the alien vocable, we had better naturalize it as *questionary*.

The secret motive which urges men otherwise estimable to wander into these linguistic aberrations is at bottom only intellectual snobbery. To the half-educated, and even to the over-educated, foreign words, foreign phrases, and foreign plurals look bigger and braver and better. To the truly educated, to those whose education has been assimilated, their own language is sufficient for all things, as adequate to the highest as to the lowest. Lincoln was no more tempted to stray outside the borders of English than Luther was to break out of the boundaries of German.

On one occasion when the late Sir Henry Irving was dining at the house of a friend in New York his attention was called to a picture of the lady of the house and the artist who was responsible for it was introduced to him. It was charming as a piece of painting but it was less satisfactory as a likeness of the sitter. Irving looked at it and compared it with the living original, standing just beneath it. Then he turned to the artist and ventured a pertinent question: "When you were painting the portrait of our charming hostess, why didn't you paint a *portrait* of our charming hostess?"

And that is the question that may be put to every one of us. When we are speaking English—why not speak English and nothing else? Why not stick to English? Why not employ only pure English?—that is to say, words whether native or imported it matters not, so long as they obey the laws of our own language. For if we persist in interlarding what we have to say with foreign phrase and foreign words, we are confessing that we have not mastered the resources of our own incomparable tongue with all its inexhaustible riches. If we bestow foreign pronunciations or foreign spellings or foreign plurals upon the words we employ, we are confessing that these words are not wholly and completely English—and if that is the case why should we employ them?

These things have often been said before and they will need to be said often again. Only by iteration and by reiteration can we bring home to all men the abiding principles which protect the purity of English against the insidious prac-

tices of the pedants and the precisians who are
prone to deal with the language as if it were
dead and who fail to perceive that if it is to be
kept alive it must obey the laws of its being.

VI

THERE are, however, not a few words of foreign origin which have made themselves at
home in English since a time whereof the memory of man runneth not to the contrary, which
therefore no stickler for purity would hesitate
to use, and which none the less, despite their
familiarity, retain an alien aroma, vague but
unmistakable.   One of these words is *rendezvous*
and another is *bouquet*. As a noun *rendezvous*
has been English for more than two centuries,
as we discover by consulting the Oxford Dictionary, and as a verb it has been English for
only a little less than two centuries. And yet—
and yet the doubt lingers whether it is really
anglicized once for all, whether it is a word of
good standing in English. For one thing, it
parades its alien origin and it retains its foreign
pronunciation. There clings to it still the flavor
of the original tongue in which it came into
being; and this flavor has a tendency to arrest
attention. No doubt it is useful, since it can
indicate a meeting appointed both as to time
and as to place. In the sense of an hour fixed

in advance, *rendezvous* has a synonym in a recently devised Americanism, *date:* "let us make a *date*." One admirer of Alan Seeger's noble lyric has even been bold enough to regret that the American poet did not dare the Americanism—"I have a date with Death!"

Probably only a very few of the many who have thrilled at the lofty eloquence of the young American poet have felt an alien accent in the use of *rendezvous*. The poem was written in France and it was written by a soldier of France; and therefore there may even be a significant propriety in this use of a French military term enrolled long ago in our English vocabulary. But can as much be said for the employment of another noun of French origin in another lofty lyric written by another American poet?

It is in the second stanza of Walt Whitman's heartfelt lament for Lincoln that we find this doubtful word:

"O Captain! my Captain! rise up and hear the bells;
  Rise up—for you the flag is flung—for you the bugle trills,
  For you *bouquets* and ribbon'd wreaths—for you the shores a-crowding,
  For you they call, the swaying mass, their eager faces turning;
    Here, Captain! dear father!
      This arm beneath your head!
    It is some dream that on the deck
      You've fallen cold and dead."

55

Now, is it hypercriticism to feel a lack of propriety, an artistic incongruity, in the use of *bouquet* in a poem on the death of Lincoln? Of course, *bouquet* is good enough English, even if its spelling parades its foreign origin. But somehow it seems out of place in Whitman's manly lines. Yet what other word could he use, after all? The older and native *nosegay* would have been even more out of keeping. It may be that *bouquet* had a better standing in English when Whitman wrote, more than half a century ago, than it has to-day, when it seems to be going out of use even in ordinary speech. In this twentieth century the lover does not send a *bouquet* to his lady-love; he sends her "a bunch of flowers." And a bunch of flowers does not evoke the idea of stiff and artificial arrangement which is more or less clearly connoted by *bouquet*.

VII

It is of good omen that there has been founded in London a "Society for Pure English." It was designed to spread abroad a knowledge of the true theory and the proper practise of the English language. It proposed to encourage "those who possess the word-making faculty to exercise it freely." It advocated the thoro anglicizing of all alien words deserving incorporation into English, thus defending the purity of English against the pedants. In the Society's preliminary pamphlet, in its declaration of principles, which is really a ringing declaration of independence from pedantry and from the false idea of purity, there are several significant passages. Here is one of these:

> As we more and more rarely assimilate our borrowings so even words that were once naturalized are being now one by one made un-English, and drawn out of the language back into the foreign forms. . . . The mere printing of such words in Italics is an active force toward degeneration.

And here is another passage as rich in good counsel:

> Believing that language is or should be democratic both in character and origin, and that its best word-makers are the uneducated, and not the educated classes, we would prefer vivid popular terms to the artificial creations of scientists. We shall often do better by inquiring, for instance, not what name the inventor gave to his new machine but what it is called by the workmen who handle it; and in adopting their homespun terms and giving them literary currency we shall help to preserve the living and the popular character of our speech.

(1914–1919.)

57

III

AMERICAN ENGLISH AND BRITISH ENGLISH

III

AMERICAN ENGLISH AND BRITISH ENGLISH

I

M RS. MALAPROP was not alone in her
anxiety about her "parts of speech" and
in her sensitiveness when aspersions were cast
upon her "nice derangement of epitaphs." To
most of us the language we have in our mouths
and at the end of our pens is always interesting
even if our attention is directed to it only occa-
sionally and only when we are suddenly surprised to discover that somebody else does not
use words exactly as we do. We are all inclined to accept our own vocabulary and our
own usages as standards by which to judge the
vocabulary and the usages of everybody else;
and we are often not a little shocked and even
grieved when we find that others do not always
accept our ways of speaking and writing as
necessarily right and proper.

When we take the trouble to analyze our own
standards we cannot help seeing that they are
first of all personal; secondly, local and sectional; and thirdly, national. I know that I

employ certain words in certain meanings and that I pronounce them in a certain fashion, first because I am the son of a Massachusetts father and of a Virginian mother; second, because I have been for now three-score years a New Yorker by residence; and thirdly, because I am an American by citizenship and not a British subject. And perhaps the more significant of my individualities of speech are not personal or sectional so much as they are national. I use either *autumn* or *fall*, whereas my cousins in England employ only the former word, their forefathers having allowed the latter to fall into innocuous desuetude. I wear a *tuxedo*, whereas my friends in London don *dinner-jackets*. And these divergencies of the everyday vocabulary of the United States from that of Great Britain seem at first glance to be so many that there is an impending danger of a splitting up of the English language into two dialects, American and British.

Among the hints prefixed to the English version of Baedeker's ' Guide to the United States' there is to be found a cautiously selected glossary, to enable the wandering Briton to translate the unaccustomed Americanism he is likely to hear into the corresponding Briticism with which he has always been familiar. And there ought to be a similar glossary in the

'Guide to the British Isles' for the benefit of the voyaging American.

We may assume that this Baedeker glossary was prepared by Mr. Muirhead, an Englishman long resident in the United States. It catalogues about a hundred instances of the divergence of vocabulary; and to the untraveled American this list is instructive; it is an aid to his understanding of imported fiction. It informs us that what we call a *bedspread* is known in England as a *counterpane*. Our *bureau* is their *chest of drawers;* our *drummer* is their *commercial traveler;* our *muslin* is their *cotton cloth;* our *calico* is their *printed cotton cloth;* and our *notions* are their *small wares.* It fails to mention our *commutation-ticket*, which is their *season-ticket*, and which has given us *commuter* to describe a resident of the remoter suburbs—a word quite incomprehensible to the Londoner. It defines Americanisms for which there are no equivalent Briticisms because the things themselves are more or less unknown in Great Britain —for example, *cowboy* and *cuspidor.* It seems to imply that we always substitute *fall* for *autumn, rooster* for *cock, deck* for *pack* (of cards), and *wilt* for *wither;* and this implication is unwarranted since we use both *fall* and *autumn, rooster* and *cock, deck* and *pack, wilt* and *wither.* And the attention of the wandering Briton might have been called to the fact that *fall* and *deck*, *rooster* and *wilt* are not new words of American manufacture; they are good old English words of honorable lineage, which our kin across the sea have allowed to die and which we on this side of the Western Ocean have kept alive.

Of course, the glossary in Baedeker's 'United States' is incomplete in its record of divided usage; probably it would be possible to add to its hundred words two or three hundred more. It omits, for example, our *farm-hand* whom the British designate as an *agricultural laborer* and our *stem-winder* which they call a *keyless watch*. And if it had been prepared for the use of American visitors to the British Isles it would have had to be enlarged to contain the Briticisms for which there are no corresponding Americanisms, because we do not happen to have the custom which called them into existence in England. There would be advantage in explaining to the American visitor that if he goes to an English hotel for a dinner at a fixed price, he will be at liberty to call for a second helping of anything which may please his palate, if the bill-of-fare declares that "a *follow* of any dish will be served without extra charge." And perhaps it might be as well to notify this same American visitor that when he chances to discover on his baggage a label containing only the strange and mysterious word *excessed*, he is to understand that this misbegotten vocable is merely a record of his having paid the extra fee for the weight of his trunks in excess of the number of pounds allowed on a single railway ticket.

The first time the voyaging American beholds a *follow* or *excessed* he is likely to be as bewildered as the wandering Briton is when he first encounters *commuter* and *cuspidor*. Yet no one of these four words, two Briticisms and two Americanisms, is to be stigmatized as slang or dismissed as dialect. On both sides of the Atlantic there are local dialects, differentiated by many departures from the standard English of literature; and both in Great Britain and in the United States slang is forever springing up overnight, flourishing for a brief season and dying unregretted. It is not to be expected that an American should be acquainted with all the local dialects of England or that an Englishman should be able to apprehend at sight the meaning of all the variegated expansions of American slang.

A New Yorker is justified in his surprize when he first overhears one cockney condemn another cockney as "a *bally* idiot"—*bally* being an adjective of reproach insistently disseminated by the unregenerate contributors to a London weekly paper, generally called *The Pink Un;* and imagination balks at the blank helplessness of a Briton if he had been called upon to explain a sentence uttered in the hearing of a friend of mine and immediately decipherable by every New Englander. It was a score of years ago in the forgotten days when young fellows used their vacations for bicycle trips in the unexplored back country. My friend went into a remote Vermont inn for his mid-day luncheon; and after the obligatory roast beef and fried potatoes he asked the waitress what there was for dessert. When she told him that he could have his choice of pie or pudding, he inquired: "What kind of pie?" To which she made answer: "Open-top, criss-cross, and covered." After due consideration my friend decided upon apple, declining custard and mince.

II

WHEN all is said that needs to be said and when we have set up a few score Americanisms over against a few score Briticisms, we cannot help seeing that the divergencies between British English and American English are relatively very few if only we keep in mind the immense vocabulary of our ever-expanding language.

These localisms are mostly colloquialisms; and they seem to be far more numerous than they really are because most of them belong to the vocabulary of everyday life—because they are familiar household words, often spoken and only infrequently written. The English of literature, and even the English of journalism, is comparatively free from local peculiarities. In the dialog of their novels Hardy and Howells necessarily make artistic use of appropriate dialect; but in their narratives, when they speak in their own persons, the English of the American is as pure and simple as the English of the Briton. Both of them have the skill to utilize all the resources of their common language; and to either of them we can apply Milton's commendatory phrase: "His words, like so many nimble and airy servitors, trip about him at command." We discover the same reliance upon the common stock of English words, the same avoidance of localisms in the leaders in the London *Times* that we find in the editorials of the *New York Times*.

So long as the novelists and the newspaper men on both sides of the ocean continue to eschew Briticisms and Americanisms and so long as they indulge in these localisms only in quotation-marks, there is no danger that English will ever halve itself into a British language and an American language. We may rest assured that all the superficial evidences of a tendency toward the differentiation of American English and British English are not so significant as they may appear to the unreflecting and that the tendency itself will be powerless against the cohesive force of our common literature, the precious inheritance of both the English-speaking peoples.

I have read somewhere that not long after we had proclaimed our independence of the English crown a perfervidly patriotic member of the Continental Congress moved that we renounce the English tongue and devise a new language of our own, a speech which we should not have to share with the enemy; and as I recall it, Roger Sherman moved as an amendment that we retain the English language and compel the British to acquire some other. Even if the original motion had slipped through without opposition, it would soon have been made evident that legislative fiat is helpless in the face of linguistic tenacity. In all the long history of mankind no people has ever coerced itself or its conquered neighbor into giving up an ancestral tongue. The roots of the mother speech are intertwined in the human soul, so inextricably that it is beyond the power of man to pluck them out.

68

It is fortunate for the citizens of the United States and for the widely scattered subjects of the British Empire that neither of the motions brought forward in the disheartening days of the Revolution, which separated these two peoples politically, that neither of the two impossible proposals could be carried into effect. The possession of a common language is a bond of unity, more potent than our joint-ownership of the common law; and for the future peace of the world nothing is more important than that British and Americans shall recognize all the immense advantages of their kinship. Even if we have fought two wars, we have not drawn the sword against one another for more than a hundred years, in spite of many occasions for quarrel and in spite of three thousand miles of undefended frontier between us and Canada.

Perhaps we may go further and say that it is also fortunate for the language itself that each half of it, the British and the American, feels itself at liberty to venture upon linguistic experiments while never relaxing its loyalty to the traditions of English. Localisms are often signs of vigor and of vitality; they are novel terms on probation as candidates for acceptance in the common speech. A language is forever using up old words and in need of new words to replace those that are dead and dying.

Americanisms and Briticisms, Canadianisms and Australianisms which we are often inclined to despise when we first see them, may come to be accepted by our children as necessary replenishments of the vocabulary. If they succeed somehow in getting a foothold in the speech of the two peoples they may in time make good the right to be received into the lexicon of literature; and if this comes to pass their humble origin will be forgotten and forgiven. They will have to struggle for existence and to battle for a place in the sun and to overcome the proper prejudices of the more fastidious of speech who have constituted themselves guardians of the language, standing at its portals with drawn swords and challenging all newcomers.

Men of letters, always very conservative in their choice of words and often unfamiliar with the laws which govern the growth of language never find it easy to acknowledge the truth of Darmesteter's pregnant saying: "Universal suffrage has not always existed in politics—but it has always existed in linguistics. In matters of language the people are all-powerful and infallible, because their errors, sooner or later, establish themselves as lawful."

III

IF we can once get ourselves to consider these localisms from this point of view and to regard them disinterestedly as possible candidates for transferal from the speech of the populace to the language of literature, we shall have abandoned the attitude of contemptuous hostility from which we are prone to look down upon all linguistic novelties. Furthermore we shall find ourselves surrendering our natural prejudice against a localism because of the locality where it sprang into being. A Briticism is none the worse because it is known only to the inhabitants of the British Isles; and an Americanism is not to be despised because it is current only in America. The question is not where it was born but whether it is worthy to live. Of course, any localism is at first more or less outlandish in the eyes of those who do not dwell in the locality where it originated; and its chance of survival and of adoption elsewhere is never strong.

Some British critics have been shrill in their denunciation of invading Americanisms; and some American critics have been colonial in their apologies for these linguistic exports. This colonialism leads these American critics to steer their course by the longitude of Greenwich and

to ignore that of Washington. They are glad
to trace, if they can, an ancient and honorable
ancestry for one or another of the Americanisms which the British critics have denounced;
but if this comfort is denied them, they are
swift to shirk all responsibility for any word or
any usage "that would have made Quintilian
gasp and stare." They are modestly unwilling
to recognize the obvious fact that Americanisms
are more likely to be vital and viable than
Briticisms, because we are a younger people,
still endowed with the energy and the ingenuity
of the pioneer.

Our localisms are, as a matter of fact, more
boldly imaginative than those observable in
Great Britain; they have more of the right
Elizabethan freshness and freedom. To call an
Italian restaurant a *spaghetti-joint* is fabulous
slang, no doubt; but it is imaginative, none the
less—it is not feeble and inept, like calling
somebody "a *bally* idiot." And it is pleasant
to be able to recall that the vernacular vigor
of many Americanisms has been courteously
acknowledged by not a few British writers.
William Archer, for one, expressed his willingness to accept, as a welcome addition to standard English, our useful phrase,—"that's the
limit"; he explained that this seemed to convey to him a shade of thought not otherwise

conveyable. It is interesting to note that the French have a colloquialism exactly equivalent, —"*c'est un comble.*"

In the sedate columns of the excellent Literary Supplement of the London *Times* I recently discovered one of our latest Americanisms, *joy-ride*, printed (it must be admitted) in quotation-marks but employed without apology and with apparent approval. When our attention is thus called to it, we can all see that *joy-ride* is indeed a good word for a bad deed; and probably the authors of the books which shall delight our grandchildren will employ it without compunction and without consciousness of its former condition of servitude as slang.

A few years ago, in reviewing one of the periodical parts of the Oxford Dictionary, a writer in the Literary Supplement of the London *Times* declared that he who wished to keep English pure (that is to say, loyal to its own genius), "recognizing in popular speech the soil from which our standard language has had its origin, and to which it must return to renew its life, will look with no unkindly eye on the vivid terms which come to us from the fields, the workshop and the sea." And we may add that this purist, who must not be a pedant, will not greatly care whether the fields, the workshop, and the sea whence these vivid terms may come, shall be guarded by the Union Jack or by the Stars and Stripes. "As he will try to keep the speech he uses in close touch with the popular vernacular, so he will use his best endeavors to prevent the growing divorce between the standard speech and the language of literature."

IV

Joy-ride is only one of a rapidly increasing group of double-barreled Americanisms, if I may so call them, new compounds put together by a swift flash of inspiration. Some of them are nouns; *spell-binder, sky-scraper, calamity-howler, strap-hanger, fool-killer, rough-rider, road-hog, grub-stake, scare-head, sky-pilot.* Some of them are adjectives: *bone-dry, bone-headed, foolproof, gun-shy, tangle-foot, foot-loose, pussy-footed.* The nouns have been formed in the same fashion as the earlier literal compounds, *sky-light, type-setter, bread-box;* but on examination they reveal themselves as not literal but figurative. To call a thing a *sky-light* is to characterize it prosaically, whereas to call a thing a *sky-scraper* is to characterize it poetically. There is the same absence of literalness in the adjectives; *pussy-footed*, for example, and *bone-headed*, are of imagination all compact.

In the making of these novel locutions their

74

unknown American manufacturers were only exercising the perennial privilege of marrying any
two words whose union promises to be fruitful.
Of late the privilege has been less frequently
exercised in Great Britain than it has in the
United States; and this British self-control in
compounding is probably due to conservative
dislike of all linguistic novelty. The contributor
to the London *Times*, from whom quotation has
just been made, suggested a clever explanation
for this reluctance to accept these verbal novelties: "Our good native compounds affect us,
to use a homely phrase,—like good new boots;
they are not comfortable until they have been
a little worn."

In his illuminating discussion of the 'Rise of
English Literary Prose,' Professor Krapp has
pointed out that in the 'Arcadia' of Sir Philip
Sidney "poetic compounds of a kind prescribed
by Renascence theorists and employed by many
Elizabethan poets, frequently occur"; and he
instances "*day-shining* stars," "*honey-flowing*
speech," "*sun-staining* excellence," and "*eye-
ravished* lover." And it is obviously not difficult to parallel each of these double-barreled
Elizabethanisms with a double-barreled Amer-
canism. That this imaginative compounding
should now be more frequent in the United
States than it is in Great Britain may be accept-

ed, if we so choose, as added evidence in behalf of the belief that on this side of the Western
Ocean we have retained a slightly larger share
of the imaginative license of the Tudor writers
than has been preserved by their direct descendants in the British Isles.

We may even venture to ascend from the
prose of Sidney to the poetry of Shakspere, if
we are seeking further support for the validity
of these compounded Americanisms, some of
them certain sooner or later to win a welcome
in the language of literature. No one can fail
to see the kinship between our *sky-scraper* and
the "*cloud-capped* towers" of the 'Tempest';
and there is a relationship almost as close between our *pussy-footed* and "these most brisk
and *giddy-paced* times" of 'Twelfth Night.'
When we are told in 'Measure for Measure'
about "a man whose blood is very *snow-broth*,"
we may companion this daring noun with *joy-
ride* and *scare-head* and *moss-back*. Other of
the innumerable instances of Shaksperean compounds are *true-fixed, trumpet-tongued, quick-
coming, mouth-honor*, and *sticking-place*. We
may be sure that Shakspere would never have
rebuked the venturesome Americans who spontaneously generated *fool-killer, sky-pilot*, and
calamity-howler. And I make no doubt that
if he could have known the skunk, he would

have been delighted with the New England euphemism, which, so Lowell told us, called that pervasive animal an *essence-pedlar*.

(1918.)

IV

THE VICISSITUDES OF THE VOCABULARY

IV

THE VICISSITUDES OF THE VOCABULARY

I

THOSE of us who really love literature cannot help having a keen relish for the dictionary. It may tempt us to desultory reading; but it is certain always to reward us if we are properly receptive and if our curiosity is as alert as it should be. We cannot consult it without an immediate increase of information; and we always find it full of "good stories," as the Scots gardener said, even if they are "unco short," as he regretfully admitted.

Of late the dictionary has been more or less diverted from its original purpose by ambitious editors; and it has been distended by all sorts of extraneous contributions, literary and graphic,—by maps and by plates of flags and of coats-of-arms, by the inclusion of historical, biographical, and geographic material. A heterogeny of miscellaneous matters attests the competitive enterprize of the publishers of the 'Century,' the 'Standard,' and the 'International'; and no doubt this comprehensive am-

81

plitude is justified by its convenience. But the abiding value of the dictionary, its excuse for being, its fount and origin, is still its catalog of words, its orderly arrangement of the verbal riches of our inexhaustible language, ever increasing as the inevitable result of the endless energy which is the chief characteristic of the race that has the English language for its mother-tongue. We take down the dictionary sometimes to look up the exact meaning of the very newest words and sometimes to ascertain the content of words so old that they are novel to most of us. And when the word we are seeking is important enough to be elucidated by illustrative quotations signed and dated, then we find both profit and pleasure in the swift revelation of its history, of its source, of its transformations, of the modifications of its meaning and of its differentiation from its synonyms. We are reminded of its precise limitations and even of its occasional misuse due to confusion with a kindred term.

When I happened not long ago to open that noble monument of linguistic research, the 'Oxford Dictionary,' I could not resist the impulse to browse up and down its compact columns, after I had found the information I was in search of; and I chanced upon the word *dictionary*, noting especially three of the illustra-

tive quotations. The first of these was a remark of Archbishop Trench in 1857 to the effect
that "a dictionary, according to that idea of it
which seems to be alone capable of being logic-
ally maintained, is an inventory of the language"; and in this remark we can find the
genesis of the 'Oxford Dictionary' itself. The
second was a characteristic utterance of Emerson's in one of the essays collected in 'Society
and Solitude' and published in 1870: "Neither
is a dictionary a bad book to read . . . it is
full of suggestion—the raw material of possible
poems and histories." And the third was taken
from a volume of 'Lectures on Preaching,' delivered by Dr. R. W. Dale in 1878: "A dictionary is not merely a home for living words; it is
a hospital for the sick; it is a cemetery for the
dead."

Dr. Dale's sentence calls attention to the
fact, often forgotten, that a dictionary must record not only the terms of to-day familiar to
all of us even if we may fail to employ them
with precision; it must also serve as an asylum
for aged and decayed words no longer strong
enough to withstand the fierce competition
which is ever visible in the vocabulary and
which is a condition precedent to the vigor and
vivacity of the language. Our attention is frequently called to the unending expansion of

English; and the dictionary-makers vie with one another in capturing every new-fledged word; they point with pride to the thousands of linguistic novelties which they have been swift to include in their latest editions.

But we do not always remember that an inventory of the language must be hospitable also to the dead and dying words, to the decrepit terms pushed out of popular favor by the onrushing throng of sturdy newcomers. Some of these striplings who insist on invading the vocabulary were born in the library or in the laboratory and some of them were generated spontaneously in the shop and in the street; but no matter where they may have been cradled they have the energy and the ambition of youth, and with the unconscious cruelty of the young they shoulder out of the way their elders and betters. They know that they are the shock troops which are essential to advance; and they have no pity for the invalid vocables who cannot even hold the line, no longer fit for service and certain to be superannuated sooner or later.

It is no matter for surprize that the publishers, as soon as they have got out one of the huge and swollen tomes in which they have vainly endeavored to include all the words of our language, dead and alive, go to work at once to get out a smaller volume to contain only the twenty or thirty thousand words which are indisputably living and which have the longest expectation of life. Many of these robust youngsters have not attained to their majority; but none the less do they thrust themselves forward and crowd aside ancient and honorable terms now too enfeebled to defend themselves in the struggle for existence.

II

THE coming in of golf brought into general use a score or more words which were novel to the average Briton and American, even if they may have long been current on the sea-shore links of Scotland. Even those of us who have never been lured into playing the ancient and honorable game, have been forced to learn its language. We are all more or less familiar with *foursomes* and with *putting-greens*, with the *brassie* and with the *tee*. But very few of us have ever had any occasion to ascertain the technical meaning of *eyas* or *rufter*, *hood* or *yarak;* and it is safe to say that scarce one widely read man in ten thousand could explain what *bewits* are or what are *varvels*. Yet these queer vocables were familiar to all who pretended to good breeding when the noble sport

85

of falconry was still in fashion. The technical terms of hawking numbered at least two or three score; and we must recapture as best we can the meaning of a few of them if we want to apprehend the full purport of certain lines of Shakspere. The gallants who sat on the stage of the Globe Theater all understood Othello when he cried out

If I do prove her *haggard,*
Though that her *jesses* were my dear heart-strings,
I'd whistle her off.

But this speech is now incomprehensible to any of the occupants of the orchestra seats of our New York playhouses,—unless by chance Rudyard Kipling happened to be one of them. He knows the special vocabulary of falconry, as he knows many another of the myriad special vocabularies which make up the English language. Not only does he understand the technicalities of hawking when he hears them, he can employ them with his customary accuracy. At least so we must believe when we note that he has prefixed to one of the chapters of 'Kim' a manufactured quotation from the dialog of an unnamed and non-existent old play:

Your *tiercel's* too long at *hack*, Sire. He s no *eyass*
But a *passage-hawk* that footed ere we caught him,
Dangerously free o' the air. Faith ! were he mine

(As mine's the glove he binds to for his *firings*)
I'd fly him with a *make-hawk*. He's in *yarak*
Plumed to the very point—so manned so weakened. . . .
Give him the firmament God made him for,
And what shall take the air of him?

Just as one sport succeeds another in popularity, ousting its predecessor from favor and then perhaps after a hundred years or more of universal vogue withdrawing into obscurity as its successor supplants it, so now and again a new science comes into prominence and compels us to acquaint ourselves with its newfangled technicalities while another science sinking into discredit carries down with it all its own special terms. In the past quarter of a century bacteriology has proved its indispensability; and we have had to learn the significance of *antiseptic* and *germicidal* and to recognize that *culture* has taken on a new meaning in addition to those it had half a century ago. But we have now no occasion to store our memories with any of the strange terms of the pseudo-science of alchemy which was losing its right to be reckoned as a science at least three hundred years ago. These strange terms, withdrawing from our everyday speech, have found refuge in the dictionary, where we have to pursue them if we wish to apprehend the richly realistic dialog of Ben Jonson's best comedy, the 'Alchemist.'

87

THE VICISSITUDES OF THE VOCABULARY

It is at least doubtful whether all the ground-
lings who stood in the open yard of the Globe
Theater, could have defined the technical terms
that the playwright employed with precision:

> Take away the *recipient*,
> And *rectify* your *menstrue*, from the *phlegma*.
> Then pour it, o'er the *Sol*, in the *cucurbite*

> Can you *sublime* and *dulcefie?* *Calcine?*
> Know you the *sapor pontick?*

But even if most of the London playgoers of
the early seventeenth century could at least
guess at the content of these words, it is certain
that every one of the New York playgoers of
the early twentieth century would confess
blank ignorance.

Yet it is never safe to assume that all the
tenants who slumber in the linguistic grave-
yard are dead and gone. There are words not
a few which have lain in the verbal necropolis
for long years and which were only sleeping, all
the while ready to awaken from their trance and
to come forth at the call of a poet who needed
their services and who summoned them again
to draw the breath of life. Lowell declared that
Emerson's "eye for a fine, telling phrase that
will carry true is like that of a back-woodsman
for a rifle; and he will dredge you up a choice
word from the mud of Cotton Mather himself."

88

Keats went back to Spenser and resuscitated from suspended animation words which Spenser in his turn had revived from Chaucer and not always with understanding. Chaucer, for example, speaks of those who *derring* (=*daring*) *do;* Lydgate misinterpreted this and Spenser misconstrued it, taking these two words for one; and so it came about that Scott and Bulwer Lytton talk about "deeds of *derringdo*." A few years ago E. B. Tylor asserted that English is "in a freely growing state, and capable of adding to itself by almost any process found in any language in the world,"—an assertion which covers its capacity to add to itself by making one new word out of two old words, joined in their own despite.

III

MORE than half a century ago, William Cullen Bryant drew up a list of the locutions of which he disapproved,—the words, the usages, the phrases that he did not wish to see in the columns of the evening paper he had edited for many years. The American poet had a fine feeling for propriety of speech and he had also a high regard for the purity of English. His qualifications for expressing linguistic prejudices were obvious; and there were many who were ready to bow to his authority in his own time. His index expurgatorius was borrowed by other editors in all parts of the country. It had its day of vogue and it was frequently invoked by the purists and the pedants who are always with us. Even now, as we approach the end of the first quarter of the twentieth century, Bryant's list remains a significant document, altho its impressiveness has departed. We can still read this catalog of a poet's likes and dislikes with profit, even if we have only a diminishing respect for his opinions. We cannot help seeing that not a few of his verbal decisions have been recalled by popular vote. Public opinion finds means to express itself and to overrule the judgments of the courts which may have tried to assert an unwarranted jurisdiction over our parts of speech. Fortunately for the vigor and for the diversity of English our energetic tongue is not under the control of scholars and schoolmasters—or even of poets.

Bryant laid his interdict upon *talented* and *reliable*, both of them accepted to-day as words in good standing, having lived down the stigma of their illegitimate birth. He objected to those malformed verbs *collide* and *donate*, both of them winning their way because they have demonstrated their utility. He insisted that *lenity* and *jeopard* should be preferred to *leniency* and *jeopardize*. Now, there is no doubt that *lenity* and *jeopard* are older and therefore more respectable

than those literary upstarts *leniency* and *jeopardize;* and we may even go farther and admit
that when we had *lenity* and *jeopard* there was no
necessity for inventing *leniency* and *jeopardize*
and no advantage in it.   None the less is it a fact
that the two later forms have substituted themselves for the two older and that the two older
have now so completely dropped out of use that
to employ them to-day would almost savor of
affectation.

In his lecture on 'English, Past and Present,'
Trench declared that the "mysterious sentence
of death which strikes words, we oftentimes
know not why, others not better, it may be
worse, taking their room, will frequently cause
in process of time, a word to perish from one
branch of a common language while it lives on in
the other."   Here in the United States we have
kept alive *fall* as a synonym for *autumn;* and
our British cousins on the far side of the Western
Ocean have allowed it to die.   We have retained
and they have dropped to *wilt* (= to *wither*
and to fade as a flower), an expressive word
which it would be a pity to lose.   We still call
a man who makes up prescriptions a *druggist*;
and our kin across the sea prefer now to call him a
chemist—which he is not.   The vocabulary of
the King James version of the Bible seems to
have influenced the current speech of New Eng-

land more deeply than it has affected the current speech of old England; and as a result many good old words, *vouchsafe*, for example, and *stalwart*, have not with us Americans the slightly archaic flavor they seem to have with the British.

On the other hand, other good old words, to *blast*, for instance, and to *bloom*, have somehow been degraded in England by misuse in objurgation and as mild substitutes for the bolder verbs of profanity. I once read in a London newspaper the assertion that no writer of our time would dare to say that "Adam led his *blooming* Eve out of her *blasted* paradise." No doubt this assertion is true of British writers, who would dread arousing incongruous reactions; and, so swiftly does slang fly across the ocean, that I do not feel at all certain that any American writer would have the courage to risk these two contaminated words in a single sentence. Perhaps just at this moment an American author would hesitate to use *fierce* in its true meaning; and both American and British men of letters have long had to forgo the employment of *awful* and *terrible*, *horrid* and *weird*, all four of them defiled by widespread misusage. Evil connotations corrupt good words.

We have retained the acclimatized *gusto* as signifying hearty enjoyment but we have let slip the more completely Anglicized *gust*, as a synonym for *taste*. Yet it had a pleasant aroma of its own two centuries ago, when one of Cotton Mather's contemporaries declared that "in his style" the author of the 'Magnalia' "was something singular and not so agreeable to the Gust of the Age."

IV

BUT dead and buried as *gust* may be there is always a possibility that a master of language may call it back from the tomb and breathe the breath of life into it again. Trench in his little book marshalled a formidable army of resuscitated words which were once given up for dead. Two centuries ago editors of Chaucer and compilers of dictionaries dismissed as having departed this life vocables as vivacious to-day as *anthem, deluge, problem, illusion, sphere, phantom, plumage*, and *shapely*. And Trench drew the conclusion that the meaning of Chaucer was more readily apprehended in the nineteenth century than it had been in the seventeenth, owing to the multitude of words which had been rescued from the morgue.

Trench himself did not always approve of these verbal revivals, finding some of them ill-advised. "Possessing *manual*," he wrote, "we need not have called *hand-book* back from an

93

oblivion of nine hundred years,"—a curious
opinion since the native *hand-book* is a more truly
vernacular word than the imported *manual*.
Nor was Trench always inspired in his prophe-
cies as to the future viability of words. He
originally delivered his lectures in 1855 and he
thought that to *burgeon* and to *sag* were then
in a moribund condition and that *dullard* and
mother-naked were in a state of decline and
likely soon to be borne away in the plumed
hearse of the verbal undertaker.

Among our kin across the sea *rooster* and *shoat*
(=a little pig) have so completely faded from
memory that our British cousins often denounce
them as abhorrent Americanisms. The British
have also allowed *chore* to go out of use, retaining it only in the modified compound *char-
woman;* and both in Great Britain and in the
United States we have been willing to let two
synonyms for *shirt* drop out of the vocabulary,—
smock and *shift*. Yet *smock* still survives in
the compound name *smock-frock* and *shift* still
survives in the adjective *shiftless,* denoting a
fellow so ineffectual that he "hasn't a shirt to
his back."

It would lead me too far afield if I were to attempt to discuss the many words which are not
actually dead or even dying, but which have lost
their honor and which live on after their fame has

been stained by degradation and disgrace. Once upon a time *libel* was only "a little book" and carried with it no connotation of personal insult; and it may be noted as curious that in French a corresponding opprobrium has been visited upon *pamphlet*, which is still only a little book in English whereas in French it now indicates a libel. The verb to *garble* has also descended in the scale; as Trench pointed out it originally meant only to *sift*, to select for the purpose of getting at the best, whereas now it implies a selection for the purpose of getting at the worst.

In Ben Jonson's time to *censure* carried with it no suggestion of disparagement. It meant only to estimate and to judge,—to express an opinion either favorable or unfavorable as the case might be. Altho Bacon (in 1625) seemed to use the word with an anticipation of its present meaning to *find fault*, declaring that he "would not *censure* or speak ill of a man," Benjamin Franklin, writing almost exactly a century later (in 1729), employed it in its older sense, expressing the hope that he might be "*censured with candor.*" A similar fate may be impending for the corresponding verb to *criticize*; in the vocabulary of literature this still indicates an unbiased exercise of the judgment; but in our every-day speech, it has come to imply *fault-finding*.

95

On the other hand to *appreciate*, which has hitherto been used to mean the making of an unprejudiced estimate, is coming to imply the expression of a favorable opinion. Perhaps this modification of the meaning of *censure, criticize,* and *appreciate* is evidence that we find it difficult to be just and dispassionate and that we tend unconsciously to be either harsher or gentler than we ought to be.

(1918.)

V

THE LATEST NOVELTIES IN LANGUAGE

V

THE LATEST NOVELTIES IN LANGUAGE

I

THE English language is an Inn of Strange Meetings. Its doors stand open always; and it extends a warm reception to travelers from foreign lands. Some of its guests are able to make themselves welcome, and they therefore settle down as regular boarders; while others, finding themselves ill at ease, restless and useless, are to be considered as transients, lodgers for the night only. The demand for accommodation has been so persistent and so imperious that the hostelry has now to keep on enlarging itself to provide for the newcomers, often to the disgust of the older guests swift to resent what they consider the intrusion of the vulgar herd; and they have cried out indignantly sometimes against the low-born native and sometimes against the undesirable alien. The vocables who vaunt their descent from the ancient and honorable Anglo-Saxon stock may be justified in their abhorrent contempt for uncouth plebeians, like *gents* and *pants*, and for inacceptable immigrants, like *artiste* and *pianiste*. But probably these verbal aristocrats would be shocked if they were to hear the Celt and the Latin protest against the term *Anglo-Saxon* itself, often denounced as inaccurate and misleading, when applied to the English language, of which the vocabulary is probably at least one half of Romance origin, or when applied to the English-speaking peoples, who have received invaluable accretions from many other races, French and Dutch, German and Scandinavian.

It must be admitted that *Anglo-Saxon*, like so many other words in everyday use in our language, is not wholly satisfactory; yet it has firmly established itself in current speech and it is more convenient than any of the other terms which have been proposed to take its place. In his brilliant and sympathetic history of English literature, M. Jules Jusserand very sensibly accepted the wider application of *Anglo-Saxon*, calling it a composite word, "which has the advantage of being clear" and which "has in its favor a long usage." Of course, the English language, strictly speaking, is Anglo-Saxon only in its bony skeleton; and a large part of the flesh which clothes its bare framework is derived from one or another of the languages into which Latin slowly modified itself in the course of the centuries following the decline and fall of the Roman Empire,—a double origin of the English vocabulary to which our noble tongue owes its extraordinary and unparalleled richness. Our language has also acclimated words from almost every other speech, ancient and modern, taking for example, *canoe* and *totem* from our American Indians, *loot* and *ayah* from the remoter Indians of Hindustan, *boss* and *stoop* from the Dutchmen who colonized New York, and *taboo* from the South Sea islanders. And by the side of these importations, English has never forgone its right to manufacture all the new words it discovers itself to need, making these out of hand, inspired by the mother of invention and aiming always at the soul of wit.

A few years ago a British reviewer of the monumental Oxford Dictionary declared that the English language has truly a "marvellous digestion and seems able to feed on almost any kind of nutriment. Popular slang and old pedantries, the dreams of philosophers and the cant of thieves, puns and perversions, forgotten fears and ancient superstitions have all contributed to its vocabulary; and some of our most respectable words have wild and strange histories; and it gives us warrant to hope that what English has done in the past to nourish its vigor, it will continue to do in the future."

We need not be alarmed if in this first quarter of the twentieth century, as in every quarter of

every other century for now a thousand years or
more, new words of all sorts and conditions are
being added to the language, springing up spontaneously often from seeds of doubtful origin.
There are so many of these verbal novelties and
they spread themselves so swiftly and so insid-
iously that very few of us are conscious of more
than a small proportion of them. In the past
decade we have learned to use *pep* and *jazz;* we
have been taught to feel a hostile contempt for
profiteers and for *hyphenated* citizens; and we
have been told what manner of man a drug-*addict*
is and what manner of thing a *fabricated* ship.
And when one or another of these intruding vocables has first fallen on our ears in the street or
come under our eyes in the study, there have not
been wanting those among us who were acutely
pained and who were ready to echo Mrs. Quickly's "Here will be an old abusing of God's pa-
tience and the King's English!"

Whether these six new words are or are not
going to be accepted into standard English and to
be employed without the apology of quotation-
marks, cannot be predicted by any one to-day.
Their acceptance will depend on their utility, not
on their regularity of construction or their legit-
imacy of descent. Dr. Henry Bradley in his
most instructive little book on the 'Making of
English' took occasion more than once to em-

phasize the fact that the "regard for correctness" is powerless "when it conflicts with the claims of convenience of expression." If a new word is recognized as meeting a need of the language, as providing an easier or a more effective way of saying something that we want to say, then its future is assured; the most perfervid protests against it will be unavailing.

II

WHERE do all our new words come from, both the feeble vocables destined to an early death and the verbal entities lively enough to force themselves into the vocabulary? Who makes them? How are they made? These are questions to which it is often difficult to find an answer. Sometimes we know who made a word, why he made it, where he made it, and when he made it. Huxley manufactured *agnostic*, from a Greek root, intending it to be a more accurate description of his own attitude toward inherited religious belief than *positivist*. It was aptly and correctly formed; it was needed; it was immediately adopted both by his friends and his foes; and from English it has made its way into most modern languages.

But where did *jazz* come from? Who was responsible for this fit name for misfit music? And when was it that some person or persons to us unknown had a happy inspiration and described syncopated measures as *rag-time?* We can make a guess that *pep* is a curtailing of *pepper* and that *boob* is only a shortened *booby*; but why is a recently invented combination of ice-cream and fruit-syrup known as a *sundae?* And why is this name not more simply spelled either *sunday* or *sundy?* Why was the armored tractor which helped powerfully to win the war entitled a *tank?* Here indeed is an instance of the way in which an old word is sometimes applied to a new thing in spite of the fact that it is not at all a good name for this invention. There is no likeness at all between a receptacle for liquids (which was the only meaning of *tank* before the Great War) and a caterpillar tractor steel-clad and bristling with guns (which is what *tank* means to-day even tho it retains also its earlier significance).

A score of years ago, during the war in South Africa, we were made familiar with the verb *to commandeer*, a needless novelty since the English language already had its exact equivalent in *to requisition;* and during the Great War were called upon to accept another new verb, *to profiteer*, framed on the model of *commandeer* (perhaps with some memory also of *privateer*) and almost as unnecessary as *commandeer*, since we might have brought into general use the law-term *to forestall.* But *forestall* does not suggest all that we think we recognize in *profiteer;* and a new word justifies its creation even when it conveys only a slight difference in meaning.

The insistent desire to save time and to shorten a polysyllable whenever this is possible has led the British to cut down *cinematograph* to *cinema* and it has led Americans to substitute *the movies* for *moving-pictures.* These truncated terms seem to have ousted their long-legged progenitors, partly no doubt because of the universal appeal of the photographic panorama,—the pressure to abbreviate a name being in proportion to the frequency of its use as well to as its original prolixity. In like manner have we shortened *taxi-meter cab* to *taxi,*—just as our forefathers exercised the same privilege and cut *cabriolet* down to *cab.* It is amusing to note that these more leisurely ancestors of ours curtailed *cabriolet* to preserve only *cab* whereas they beheaded *periwig* to preserve only *wig,* while we ourselves seem almost as ready to chop the head off *telephone* and the tail off *photograph.*

Rudyard Kipling, always fastidious in his use of English, has no hesitation in employing *photos* (in 'Kim'); and the managers of the moving-picture theatres invite us to behold *photo-plays,* a violent barbarism of immediate utility. Kipling cannot escape the ultimate responsibility for another abbreviated word, which has taken its place in the technical vocabulary of the so-called "silent drama." His biting lyric on the 'Vampire,' with its corroding characterization of its heroine- villainess as "a rag and a bone and a hank of hair," has brought about a belief that a vampire is always the female of the species; and as a logical result of this unfounded opinion any fascinating adventuress trying to cajole an innocent hero is now entitled a *vamp*. What is even more picturesque is that this abbreviated noun has also become a verb: "She *vamps* him."

This is an excellent example of that striving for "elliptic brevity" which Dr. Bradley has called a striking characteristic of spoken English. Dr. Bradley also pointed out that "the tendency to reduce the number of syllables in words wherever it was possible" can be discovered in our language as early as the fifteenth century. It is one of many forces forever at work to bestow on the English language the simplicity and the directness, the efficiency and the energy, which the English-speaking peoples continually display in the other relations of life. Every race makes its language of its own image; and as soon as we have grasped the governing principles of the growth of this language of ours, we have acquired an insight into the psychology of the two peoples whose mother-tongue it is.

When we feel that the undue length of a word unfits it for the swift transaction of business, we may now and again seek to find a short, sharp substitute, as when we say *to wire* instead of *to telegraph*. But more often than not the long word is itself mercilessly abbreviated, as when *advertizement* is reduced to *ad*. Then we go a little further and describe a two-line advertizement under the general head of Help Wanted as a "want *adlet*." And there are those who are willing to adventure themselves still further along this path of linguistic efficiency and designate the advertizing expert as an *ad-smith*, a novel locution (still unknown to our kin across the sea), which Howells immediately hailed as "delightful," thereby vindicating his inexpugnable Americanism. True it is he went on to remark that *ad* "is a loathly little word, but we must come to it. It's as legitimate as *lunch*,"— which we condensed from *luncheon* and which we promptly made to serve also as a verb.

III

DR. BRADLEY called attention to a device which has enriched English from time to time and which is not utilized in any other language, so far as I know. This is what is called "back-forma-tion." For example the word *grovelling* was misunderstood as a present participle and the verb *to grovel* was formed from it. So "the noun *pedlar* is older than the verb *to peddle* or the adjective *peddling*"; and the noun *editor* seems to have been the parent of the verb, *to edit*. In like manner the adjective *swashbuckling* has been deduced from the noun *swashbuckler*. "Many of the words which have been formed by this process," so the learned but unpedantic linguist assured us, "are so happily expressive that the misunderstanding that has given rise to them must be accounted a fortunate accident."

It is evidence of his freedom from pedantry that Dr. Bradley seemed to be willing to accept *to buttle*, from *butler*, *to bant* from *Banting*, the name of the Englishman who proposed a new method for reducing fat, and *to maffick*, that is to indulge in a riotous demonstration in the street, like that which took place in London in 1900 when there came the glad news of the relief of Mafeking, long beleaguered by the Boers. As Dr. Bradley passed no condemnatory verdict on these three British innovations, it is odd that he failed to mention a fourth which has won as wide an acceptance in the United States as in Great Britain,—*to burgle*, a verb back-formed from the noun *burglar* and first revealed to the world in Gilbert's brisk lyric which told us that "when the enterprising burglar isn't burgling, he likes to hear the little brook a-gurgling."

In the devising of back-formations we Americans have not lagged behind our British cousins; at least they have accused us of making the verb *to collide* out of the noun *collision,* on the erroneous assumption that as *elision* was formed from *elide,* so *collision* must have been formed from a non-existent *collide.* But if *to edit* had been made to order from *editor,* why should not *to collide* be made from *collision?* *Collide* seems now to have lived down the scandal about its unhappy past; and so has *talented,* which was once cast into outer darkness, probably because it seemed to imply a non-existent verb, *to talent.* William Cullen Bryant excluded from his newspaper another back-formation, *to donate* from *donation;* but failed to pronounce an edict of expulsion upon *to orate* from *oration.* Possibly *to orate* may not have reared its grisly head within range of the poet's vision. Even now, *to orate* is rarely used, although it has a distinct utility in that it suggests a false and flamboyant speech-making, quite different from the eloquence of a true orator.

I hesitate to conjecture what Bryant would have said if he could have heard one of the most recent of American back-formations,—the verb to be *peeved,* derived from the adjective *peevish;*

but I make no doubt that Howells would welcome it as heartily as he did *ad-smith*. Assuredly "he was *peeved*" is a delightful phrase, more subtly suggestive than "he was *peevish*," and even a little differentiated in meaning from its elder brother. While I have only cordiality for *peeved*, I wonder a little whether I should be justified in giving so hearty a greeting to a corresponding word which fell not long ago from the lips of a friend. "I won't say that my uncle was always penurious," he remarked, "but I must admit that now and again he did *penure* a little."

There is another American back-formation that I detest—*to enthuse*. I do not know why I have so bristling a repugnance to this, as I am well aware that it is no worse made than *to peeve* or *to burgle;* but somehow it seems to me vulgar and uncouth, bearing the bend sinister of offensive illegitimacy. To my mind it demands immediate deportation as an undesirable citizen of the vocabulary. I know well enough that my predjudice is probably unduly exaggerated; and I can only fall back on "I do not like you, Dr. Fell: the reason why I cannot tell." A friendly British newspaper man who came over here during the war to report on what he called 'New America,' found stimulation in the "nuggety word-groupings which are the commonplaces in good American conversation" and which "are like flashes of crystal." He noted that "Americans are never tired of bursting the bonds of convention, but when the less disciplined do this they are apt to emerge on a stage where freedom, though delightful, has its disadvantages." And my eyes are blinded to the advantages of *to enthuse*,—if there are any.

Back-formations are generally caused by the desire to save time, to cut across lots. It is swifter to call a man a *coke-fiend* than to say that he was in the habit of taking cocaine. It is sharper to declare that he is an *addict* than to describe him as addicted to indulgence in dangerous drugs. *Addict* and *coke* are to be companied with *dope*, a strange flower which bloomed in the American vocabulary only within the last decade or two of the nineteenth century and which in the first two decades of the twentieth century burgeoned exuberantly. As it happens I can recall exactly when I first became acquainted with this linguistic weed. In 1893, at the Chicago Exhibition I was told that the trained animals in the Hagenbach show were not *doped*. I immediately accepted *dope* as derived somehow from *opium* or *opiate*, altho I am still at a loss to understand how it acquired its initial.

In ensuing years I began to hear men assert that they felt *dopy*, *i. e.*, sluggish, as though they had taken an opiate. A little later the word took on an enlarged meaning, "I *doped* it out," that is to say, "I came to a conclusion." After a while I noted that a person seeking information would ask to be supplied with the *dope*. When we went to war with Germany the the American ambassador left Berlin carrying a small bag, which he held fast, because as he explained it contained the *dope* for the book he intended to write. I am watchfully waiting, eager to record any further enlargements of meaning this chameleon word may be about to acquire, assured in advance that its future cannot be more surprizing than its past.

Altho back-formation has been at work in our language for several centuries it has been more active of late in the American variety of English than in the British, because we are more inclined to take short-cuts. Some of our back-formations are abhorrent and some are appealingly picturesque even if they are also pert. "The American tongue," we are told by the wandering Briton from whom I have already quoted, "is a potent and penetrating instrument, rich in new vibrations, full of joy as well as shocks for the unsuspecting visitor." To be *peeved* is a joy even if *to enthuse* is shocking; and it must be confessed that many of our local back-formations still smack of the slums where they were born. Only one or two have been invited upstairs into the library for the use of men of letters. Yet if the rest of them may have to linger long on the threshold or even at last to be turned from the open door, they came into being in accord with the logic of our language, with its eager insistence on energetic efficiency.

IV

NEW words are derived from all sorts of sources. *To bluff*, for example, which began life as a necessary technical term in poker, spread into general use in the United States, voyaged over the Western Ocean and established itself in Great Britain, and has now crossed the English Channel and forced its admission into French and Italian and German. Perhaps *to pass the buck*, having a similar origin, will in time attain to a similar world-wide acceptance. *To spoof*, a Briticism originating in the sporting circles of London, bids fair to be adopted in New York, altho its attractiveness is as slight as its utility. Equally unnecessary is *forelady*, which is intended to be a more elegant appellation for a forewoman and which seems to presage a companion *foregentleman*—or would it be *foregent?* In another new word which we owe also to the busy marts of trade we can note again the ability of our language to supply itself easily with a term needed for immediate use. We have long been familiar with *salesman* and *saleswoman,*—even alas, with *saleslady;* and the latest member of the family to whom we have been introduced is *salesperson,* a name intended to apply to an employee of either sex.

The latest importation from France that I have had occasion to remark is no more than the conferring of a new meaning upon an old word. In English *to intrigue* has hitherto meant to plot surreptitiously, whereas in French it is used (by extension) to indicate the state of puzzled doubt in which we may find ourselves when we have reason to suspect a surreptitious plot; and this secondary French meaning is now passing over into English, so that we may read in the light stories that run through our magazines, "She *intrigued* me," meaning that she puzzled me and not meaning that she involved me in an intrigue. This Gallic secondary meaning will probably force itself into our yielding Anglo-Saxon, and we shall have hereafter the privilege of employing *to intrigue* in either of two different intents. I doubt if this will be to the profit of the language.

It is both futile and foolish for the respecter of the ancient landmarks of language to deny that an old word can have any other than its original content. The real meaning of a word is what it means now to those who utter it and to those who hear it, and not what it meant to their mothers. "There are few true synomyms in literature, none perhaps," said Dr. Clifford Allbut in his illuminating 'Notes on the Composition of Scientific Papers,' and he added that "words have not only their stem meanings, but carry upon them also many changes and tinctures of past uses, which blend inevitably in our sentences. The word *apostate*, for example, means far more than an absentee or a dissenter, and a *muscle* is much more than a little mouse; *monks* rarely live alone; your *anecdote* is anything but clandestine; *rivals* contend for other than water-rights; and *hypocrites* are no longer confined to the theater." And we cannot doubt that there were pedants who foresaw the impending degradation and the ultimate destruction of English if *apostate* and *muscle*, *anecdote* and *rival* were not each of them cribbed, cabined and confined to the single meaning justified by their derivation.

Perhaps I am playing the part of the pedant when I feel inclined to protest against the unidiomatic wording of the Covenant of the League of Nations. Apparently the phrasing of this agreement was due to a drafting clerk who had to think in two languages at once and who translated from French into English without due regard to the purity of his native tongue, —if this was in fact English. In Article 1 it is prescribed that "declarations must be deposited with the *secretariat*," when it would be purer English to specify the secretary's office. In Article 10 we are told that the Council shall *advise* upon certain matters, and the content makes it plain that the Council is not to advise some other body but itself to take action, (and this is in accord with the meaning of *aviser* in French and not in accord with the meaning of *advise* in English).

In Article 37 we read that German *nationals* in certain territory transferred to Belgium will be entitled to *opt* for German nationality— *nationals* being used for citizens and *opt* for choose. In Article 1 of the annex to the treaty of peace, permission is given to the French to *exploit* certain roads and railways, altho *exploit* in English carries a somewhat sinister suggestion absent from the French *exploiter*. In the same article we find *personnel*, meaning the workmen. In Chapter 3, there is provision for a *plebiscite*, which is what we call a referendum; and there is a mention of a *gendar-*

116

merie, which is what we call a police-force. A little later in this document we are told that a special convention will determine the conditions of payment of indemnities "to persons who have been *evacuated.*"

By some of its advocates the Covenant of the League of Nations has been likened to the Constitution of the United States; but it would be idle to deny that the new document is far inferior in its wording to the old instrument drawn up by our wise forefathers, shrewd and farseeing men who knew exactly what they wanted to say and who spared no pains to express this with the utmost concision consistent with the utmost clarity. They even went so far as to refer their draft to a special committee on style, with Gouverneur Morris as its chairman. It is greatly to be regretted that those who were responsible for the Covenant did not follow the example of those who were responsible for the Constitution.

(1919.)

VI

NEWSPAPER ENGLISH

VI

NEWSPAPER ENGLISH

I

IN the Sanskrit drama, so we are told, only
gods and heroes were allowed to use Sanskrit,
which was a highly artificial court-language, the
women and the subordinate characters being
generally limited to Pali, which was the vernacular of everyday intercourse. In Shakspere's plays, as we know, (and perhaps most
obviously in 'Julius Caesar'), the heroic figures utter their inmost thoughts in lofty and
stately blank verse, the less important personages have to content themselves with rhythmic
prose, while the illiterate rabble does the best
it can with the commonest words, without
imaginative adornment and without poetic
measure.

These were conventions of the drama in India
and in Elizabethan England long, long ago;
and yet we can find a parallel here and now in
the divergence between the language of the
lecture-hall and the language of the market-
place. The practise which delights us on the
stage is often disquieting when we observe it

outside the theater. Whenever there is a literary class there is likely to arise a literary caste, taking pride in its aristocratic aloofness and thinking scorn of the speech of the people. This literary caste tends to develop a dialect of its own, abounding in words rich in literary associations; and often it hesitates to make use of the homely terms of the unlettered.

When Jared Sparks first edited the correspondence of George Washington he was shocked to find Israel Putnam called "Old Put"; and as this familiarity seemed to him inconsistent with the dignity of history, he corrected Washington's lapses from a more scholarly standard and for "old Put" he substituted "General Putnam." Samuel Johnson was constantly on the watch to amplify the terse and unpedantic expressions natural to him and to disguise them in ornate and redundant polysyllables. Like the Yankee he wanted to prove that "I can talk long-tailed if I choose." Very few of the most renowned orators have ever approached the noble simplicity of Abraham Lincoln, to whom dignity was instinctive and who could make the lowliest words serve his purpose.

In his address on the 'Relations between Spoken and Written Language,' Dr. Henry Bradley drew attention to a peculiar and disquieting condition in the English of the present time. "Among peoples in which many persons write and read much more than they speak, the written language tends to develop more or less independently of the spoken language. In English, owing to historical causes, this process has gone farther than in other languages, so that we have the unique phenomenon of a literary vocabulary, of which a large part has no connexion with oral vernacular, but has been developed in writing by the process of transcribing the written forms of words of foreign languages. Many of the words so formed have come into popular oral use, but a vast number of them are hardly ever pronounced except in reading aloud." Dr. Bradley does not provide any examples. I venture to suggest that *irrefragable* would serve as well as any. Perhaps only a little less unlikely to have ever been actually heard by the average reader are *habitude* and *irredeemable*, and yet both are not unfamiliar to the eye.

In English, therefore, oftener than in any other language, is there danger of a more or less immediate divorce between the vocabulary of the artist and that of the artisan, between the written word and the spoken word. That this divorce has not already been decreed in England is due in part to the influence of Shak-

spere and of the English Bible; and if this influence shall ever weaken, the last state of
English will be worse than the first. There
is another influence, so Mr. Talcott Williams
has insisted, which is now being exerted,—the
influence of the newspaper both in the United
States and Great Britain, an influence which
does what it can to prevent any widening of
the breach between the unduly fastidious
language of the library and the casually careless language of the sidewalk.

Newspaper English has often been denounced
and derided; and the newspaper itself has been
called a chief among the many corrupters of
English. Mr. Talcott Williams does not waste
time in defending newspaper English; he contents himself with dwelling on its merits; and
he makes out a good case. He tells us that when
the men of letters cease to use the speech of
everyday life, the speech which is forever refreshing itself from new sources under new impulses,
the result is "a mummied tongue," whereas
"so long as accepted and acceptable writing
accepts and shares the daily changes of the
vocabulary of the market-place, so long as
both live and move and have their being in
the sun of passion, action and achievement,
the more lasting, pungent, and penetrating is
the literature of the period." And he praises

the newspapers of the British commonwealth and of the United States because they have been hospitable to "the illegitimate verbal offspring of the street, born on the wrong side of the blanket." He calls the humorous columns of our American papers "a sort of bedding-bench where the new phrases and words of the hour are set out as the gardener beds and pots young plants before they go to live in the garden-beds with an older bloom." He holds that the modern newspaper is doing its duty "in preventing a great tongue from being divided into a language of the past for letters [*i. e.*, literature] and a language of the present for common and daily use, neither sharing the life of the other."

II

In his suggestive and stimulating book, 'Literature in a Changing Age,' Professor Thorndike is as emphatic in his praise of the newspaper and of its English as is Mr. Talcott Williams. He notes that "the extension of reading is usually charged with a lowering of standards; De Quincey protested that the newspapers were encouraging long, loose, slovenly sentences; but his particular criticisms have scarcely been justified," since "newspaper English on the whole has been simple, clear and vigorous." In a later chapter Professor Thorndike asks, "Is not the newspaper, so crowded with human living, so vivid in its expression of the emotion and thought of the hour, itself a pageant that honors man's gift of expression, a triumph of his art?" And the power of the press is set forth forcibly on another page of 'Literature in a Changing Age': —"The kind of things that people like to read about, the standard of prose style, the basis of common knowledge on which imaginative writing must be premised, the guidance of good taste and manners, all these depend in the large not on one poet or all the dramatists or any master of prose or half-a-dozen moralists, but on the thousands who write the daily news and comment."

It is true that there are newspapers, and only too many of them, which delight in describing the kind of things that people ought not to like to read about, which are themselves pitiably lacking in good taste and good manners, and which do not aspire to a severe standard of prose style; but these lewd journals of the baser sort are not important or significant. In some newspapers of a more worthy type there is often a free and easy breeziness, more especially in the sporting pages, which are sometimes so bespattered with technicalities as to be unintelligible to the uninitiated. And even in the best of the newspapers of New York and London there is at times a tendency to overemphasis and to a somewhat too ponderous treatment of the often trivial happenings of the day, the incidents and accidents which must ever be the stuff and substance of journalistic chronicle and of journalistic commentary. There is a tendency to use a sledge-hammer to "swat the fly." But any one who can recall the newspapers of fifty years ago, or who has had occasion to consult their files, will bear witness to the improvement which has taken place in the past half-century.

It is nearly three score years since Lowell wrote the ever delightful discussion of the Yankee dialect, prefixt to the second series of the 'Biglow Papers.' He told us then what we need to have retold to us, generation after generation, that we are in danger of being made to talk like books "by the Universal Schoolmaster, who does his best to enslave the minds and the memories of his victims to what he esteems the best models of English composition, that is to say, to the writers whose style is faultily correct and has no blood warmth in it," since "no language after it has faded into *diction*, none that cannot suck up the feeding juices secreted for it in the rich mother earth of common folk, can

bring forth a sound and lusty book." Then
he added that "while the schoolmaster has
been busy starching our language and smooth-
ing it flat with the mangle of a supposed classical authority, the newspaper has been doing
even more harm by stretching and swelling it to
suit his occasions."

Lowell supported this last accusation by
fearsome instances, *i. e.*, "Tendered him a ban-
quet" for "asked him to dine"; "commenced
his rejoinder" for "began his answer"; the
"individual was precipitated" for the "man
fell;" "the conflagration extended its devastat-
ing career" for the "fire spread;" and "his spirit
winged its way into eternity" for "he died."
Lowell declared that he had begun to collect
these Horrible Examples before the Civil War;
and it may be doubted whether he could have
gathered such a nosegay of flowers of rhetoric
from the newspapers of thirty years later.
Certainly he could not pluck another bunch
from the journals of either New York or London
in the opening decades of this twentieth century. Probably the reporters of Lowell's
youth believed that they achieved a superior
impressiveness by an exaggerated imitation of
Dickens at his worst; and the reporters of our
time are under the more wholesome influence
of Charles A. Dana, who, whatever his sins as

an editor, knew what good English was. Mr. Talcott Williams tells us that Dana "had no hesitation in the use by his staff of any two-fisted phrase of the streets so it did its work." In other words, Dana recognized the truth of another remark of Lowell's in this same essay: "Vulgarisms are often only poetry in the egg." I confess that I have sometimes wondered what the poet who wrote the 'Biglow Papers' would have thought of the prose master who wrote 'Fables in Slang.'

Mr. Talcott Williams thinks that Benjamin Franklin set the standard style for the American newspaper, and that he saved us from the evil influence of Samuel Johnson. Professor Thorndike points out that at the very moment when De Quincey was denouncing the British journals of his time, Cobbett was revealing himself as a master of nervous English. And Father Donnelly, S. J., in his interesting book on the 'Art of Interesting,' asserts that "Macaulay, of all English writers, contributed most to the making of the language of the journalist. Macaulay gave swiftness to the English language. . . . Macaulay's style is light-footed."

Whether they are treading the trail of Franklin, with his clarity and his common sense, of Cobbett with his terseness and his sharpness, or of Macaulay with his light-footed swiftness, the journalists of to-day, reporters as well as editorial writers, are on the right road and are forever in quest of the swift word, the simplest and the boldest. It is in the writers in our periodicals, daily and weekly and monthly, rather than in the writers of our books, that we find the greater willingness to "suck up the feeding juices secreted in the rich mother earth of common folk." In the bright lexicon of journalism there are few bookish words, few "inkhorn terms," as they were called by the men of old. No doubt, our journalists tend to suck directness rather than delicacy, yet their forthright starkness rarely leads them into violence or even vehemence,—except in the stress of a presidential campaign. Probably they would satisfy the severe taste of Stendhal, who—so we are told by Mérimée,—"despised mere style and insisted that a writer had attained perfection when we remember his ideas without recalling his phrases."

III

To say this is not to say that all the newspapers of the United States and of Great Britain are always and everywhere models of styles. Far from it; even now there is bad writing of varying degrees of badness, in the editorial

columns as well as in the news pages; there is
too much of it, even if there is far less than there
was once upon a time. Especially are there
futile strivings to be humorous and strenuous
efforts to be pathetic. Humor has its place in
the newspaper as it has in life; but we resent
having serious matters presented with futile
facetiousness by reporters, and more particularly by head-line writers upon whom nature
has not bestowed a sense of humor. Of all
sad words of tongue or pen, the words of labored jocularity are perhaps the saddest. If
there is anything sadder it is the premeditated
assault upon primitive sentiment, such as we
are likely to find in the wilfully pathetic articles
of the "sob-sisters,"—as they have been happily named,—misguided ladies who strive to
out-Dickens the Dickens of blank verse death-
beds and who ask us to shed saltless tears over
the pitiful lot of amiable assassins.

Then there are the freakish tricks played
upon our unresisting language by the perpetra-
tors of scare-heads, struggling to put infinite
riches in a little room and feeling themselves
compelled to the use of abrupt words of the
needful brevity in place of the more appropriate
terms too long for the line of type. In their com-
pressed vocabulary an investigation is a *probe*,
a cross-examination is a *quiz*, and its victim is

grilled. Stolen jewelry is entitled *gems;* and a treaty becomes a *pact*. If two politicians wrangle we are told that they *clash*. This is bad enough, but worse remains behind. Men *protest* an action, instead of protesting against it; they *inquire* instead of inquiring about; and they *battle* the police instead of battling with the police.

In one of Mr. Irwin Cobb's revelatory tales of newspaper life he introduces to us an editor who "thought in head-lines" and who was therefore "drawn to individuals with short names and instinctively disliked individuals with long names." Mr. Cobb tells us that if this editor had to handle the account of the death of a tenement-house child beneath the wheels of a trolley-car, he would order it to appear with this scare-head: "Tiny Tot with Penny Clutched in Chubby Hand Dies 'Neath Tram Before Mother's Eyes." This is absurdly veracious; and attention may be called to two characteristic details—the beheading of *beneath* to *'neath* and the use of the Briticism *tram* for the Americanism *trolley* merely because the alien word is briefer by three letters.

Mr. Cobb represents his hero as working on a paper in one of our smaller cities; but I am afraid that this man has lately been promoted

to one of our metropolitan journals. If he is
not now engaged on the paper I have in mind,
then he must have a twin brother with iden-
tical idiosyncrasies. In fact, he must be one
of a large family all holding down fat jobs and
recklessly maltreating our helpless language;
and his evil influence has been denounced by
Mr. E. P. Mitchell, the editor of the brisk and
brilliant paper upon which Charles A. Dana
impressed his personality. Mr. Mitchell was
cutting in his analysis of the immediate peril
of the language. "The head-line is more influ-
ential than a hundred chairs of rhetoric in the
shaping of future English speech. There is
no livelier perception than in the newspaper
offices of the incalculable havoc being wreaked
upon the language by the absurd circum-
stance that only so many millimeters of type can
go into so many millimeters' width of column.
Try it yourself and you will understand why
the fraudulent use of so many compact but
misused verbs, nouns, and adjectives is being
imposed on the coming generation. In its
worst aspect, head-line English is the yellow
peril of the language."

No doubt what Mr. Mitchell said needed
to be said; and the warning he sounded ought
to be heeded. But even if he did not mis-
state his case, I venture to think that he a

little overstated it. Fortunately the unholy passion for abbreviating words or for employing brief words by wrenching them from their proper use is still confind to the dialect of the head-lines. These abhorrent usages show no tendency to spread down into the articles over which the head-lines display themselves like a resplendent electric sign on top of a two-story tax-payer. We may hope that the vogue of of this fashion will be fleeting, for there would be a painful corruption of the language if it should be taken up by the readers of the papers which have succumbed to the allurements of this linguistic monstrosity. Strange indeed would be the condition of our language if many of us began to talk about Tiny Tots, Quizzes and Grills, Probes and Pacts. And yet, even if that condition came to pass, it would not long seem strange. The language would make the best of a bad case, as it has done many a time and oft; and in a generation or two or three, only specialists in the history of English would know that the case had ever been bad.

That there are other infelicities in newspaper practise need not be denied,—indeed it could not be denied. The only wonder is that there are not more of them, because there is an ever-present temptation for a journalist to write journalese, to be subdued to what he works in, to content himself with the well-worn words, with the threadbare epithets, with the second-hand and third-rate commonplaces and conventionalities, flavorless and innutritious. "The daily risk of newspapers and the individual newspaper is that it will have an editorial dialect of its own," so Mr. Talcott Williams admits, and that "reporting will become reportese."

When we take into consideration the necessary rapidity with which newspaper men have to do their work and the impossibility of revision under which they labor, the wonder is not that they fall from grace now and again but that they are able to maintain an acceptable average. At times they may be unduly colloquial; but on the other hand they are very rarely pedantic. If they do not always draw from the well of English undefiled, at least they let down their buckets into the ever-flowing springs which continually refresh the speech of the people. And most of them obey the law laid down by George Henry Lewes in his instructive series of papers on 'Success in Literature': "Never rouge your style: trust to your native pallor rather than cosmetics."

(1920.)

135

VII

THE PERMANENT UTILITY OF DIALECT

VII

THE PERMANENT UTILITY OF DIALECT

I

IN the fourth volume of his history of the 'Renascence in Italy,' John Addington Symonds translated a significant passage from a letter from Filelfo, an erudite scholar, written to a friend in 1477. "I will answer you, not in the vulgar language, as you ask, but in Latin, our own true speech; for I have ever an abhorrence for the talk of grooms and servants, equal to my detestation of their life and manners. You however call that dialect vernacular, which when I use the Tuscan tongue I sometimes write. All Italians agree in praise of Tuscan. Yet I only employ it for such matters as I do not choose to transmit to posterity. Moreover, even that Tuscan idiom is hardly current thruout Italy, while Latin is far and wide diffused thruout the habitable world."

The "vulgar language," which Filelfo thus summarily dismissed, was Italian, already ennobled by the use Dante and Petrarch and

Boccaccio had made of it. This scornful attitude of a scholar of five centuries ago in regard to the language of his own country can be paralleled to-day in the attitude taken by many a man of letters toward the local dialects out of which his own language has been evolved. He holds these several dialects in sovereign contempt; he fails to see any merit in them or any value; he looks down rather intolerantly upon attempt to utilize these rusticities in verse or in prose; and he would not hesitate to echo the opinion expressed by Sir Philip Sidney in the 'Apologie for Poetry,' more than three hundred years ago: "The 'Shepherd's Calendar' hath much poetry in his eclogues; indeed worthy the reading, if I be not deceived. That same framing of his style to an old rustic language I dare not allow, sith neither Theocritus in Greek, Virgil in Latin nor Sannazar in Italian did affect it."

Moreover a man of letters, even tho he may have taught himself how to use language with delicate precision, has rarely had occasion to learn its history or to acquaint himself with the laws of its growth; and he is therefore prone to consider a dialect as a corruption of standard speech, an opinion for which there is no warrant. A true dialect is never a corruption, quite the contrary. As a cauliflower has been called "only a cabbage with a college education," so we may describe standard speech as only a dialect which has enjoyed the advantages of post-graduate instruction.

In all modern languages—and no doubt in all ancient languages also—the standard speech is but the ripe development of a dialect which was originally local to a restricted area. Italian is an evolution from Tuscan as Spanish is evolution from Castilian. And our superb and spreading English is rooted in the speech of the Midlands. If London had not been the capital of England and if Chaucer had not chosen the vocabulary of the Londoners with which to write the 'Canterbury Tales,' English would be a very different tongue from what it is. If Edinburgh had been the capital of Great Britain, Shakspere would have had to employ the broad Scots of Burns; and if Dublin had been the capital of the British Isles, the center of political power and the focus of literature, we Americans might to-day be speaking with a rich brogue.

Whenever a local dialect is slowly elevated to the rank of a language fit for literary use, it immediately begins to draw upon the neighboring dialects of the same stock for the words and the usages for which it feels a need. Thus Attic Greek enriched itself by taking over a heterogeny of locutions from Ionic Greek. Yet we can see that it is the original local dialect, of Athens or Paris, Florence or London, which is ever the sturdy trunk from which all the later foliage has burgeoned. And perhaps it is natural enough that those who profit by the spreading branches should give little thought to the roots from which it draws its strength.

Part of the neglect of the underlying dialect of a standard speech is due to the desire of the users of this speech that it shall be completely standardized, whereby pressure is ever exerted to abandon the words and to eradicate the usages which seem to be provincial or even parochial, and therefore not in accord with the relative universality of the language. Localisms are to be extirpated remorselessly; and to this schoolmasters devote themselves relentlessly. This is not only justifiable, it is judicious and even necessary. We speak with the desire to be understood; and when we make use of a localism not familiar to our hearers we arrest their attention for the moment and divert it from the matter of our remarks to the manner. We interfere with what Herbert Spencer aptly entitled the Economy of Attention.

In Goethe's autobiography he tells us how painfully he felt the pressure exerted upon him to give up pithy phrases which savored of the soil. "I had been born and bred to use the Upper-German dialect, and altho my father always cultivated a certain purity of language and early called the attention of his children to what may be regarded as the defects of that idiom, preparing us thus for better speech, I still retain certain deep-seated peculiarities of which I had grown fond. The Upper-Germans, and particularly those who live near the Rhine and and the Main (great rivers, like the seacoast, diffuse general animation), are fond of expressing themselves in similes and allusions; and they clothe sound commonplaces in apt proverbs. Such language is sometimes blunt, tho never out of place, considering its intent. . . . Every province loves its own dialect, for, properly speaking, the soul draws from it its very life-breath. . . . I was made aware that I ought to eschew the use of proverbs, which, instead of beating about the bush, always hit the nail on the head. . . . My inmost heart was, as it were, struck dumb; and I scarcely knew how to express the commonest things."

It is in consequence of this persistent intolerance of all local linguistic vagaries, of all dialectal variations from the norm of the standard speech, which is used in all official intercourse, employed almost exclusively in literature and insisted on by the schoolmasters, that Barrie's young Scotsman engaged in an unending struggle to master the artificial and unnecessary distinctions between *will* and *shall* in the first person and in the third,—distinctions which obtained in the London dialect out of which standard English has been developed and which did not obtain in the rival dialect of Edinburgh. No doubt, there are a host of ambitious young people in the United States south of Mason and Dixon's Line, who are to-day striving to compel their tongues not to say *you all*, in sentences from which those born north of that line are in the habit of omitting the *all*.

The vain efforts of the young Scotsman and of the young Southerners would have had Goethe's sympathy. He distrusted the "consolidation of the various German dialects as a means of promoting national unity"; and he esteemed dialect highly as "a perfectly legitimate outgrowth of youthful impressions and of the concurrence of the organs of hearing, speech, and thought."

II

OUR language owes its marvellous variety of vocabulary to the fusing of the Teutonic Anglo-Saxon with the Romance Norman-French; and it can preserve the necessary balance be-

tween these two constituents only by refusing
to allow itself to be unduly distended by an
excess of new vocables from either source.
The scales were depressed in the eighteenth
century by the ponderous Latinizing of Dr.
Johnson and of his obsequious and supera-
bundant disciples. Dr. Johnson himself thought
in the vernacular and then deliberately disguised this by elephantine sesquipedalianism.
He once remarked of the 'Rehearsal' that "it
had not wit enough to keep it sweet," which
was as well put as it was witty; and then he
repented of his instinctive use of the mother-
tongue and declared that the play "has not vitality enough to preserve it from putrefaction."
This second version is as wilful as it is woful;
and Macaulay was not overstating the case
when he declared that all Dr. Johnson's
books "are written in a learned language, in a
language which nobody hears from his mother
or his nurse, in a language in which nobody
ever quarrels, or drives bargains, or makes
love, in a language in which nobody even
thinks."

Then in the second half of the nineteenth
century, not long after the language had freed
itself from the Johnsonian obsession, the scales
were again weighted down on the same side
by the sudden emergence and surprizing ex-

pansion of science, which emptied into English thousands of new names for new things, taken over more or less haphazard from Latin and Greek. Many of these technical terms have passed into everyday speech and are easily comprehended of all men; they have escaped from the laboratory and the study to make themselves at home in the drawing-room ånd in the street. But many more remain in the sole possession of the little group of specialists who compounded them to serve their own necessities; and so it is that the treatises of these specialists are incomprehensible to all but their fellow specialists. The philosophers of old were able to expound their deepest thoughts without going outside the language of the average educated man; and M. Bergson and the late William James have shown us that this feat is still possible of accomplishment to-day, even if it is now a rarity. But a large majority of those who are peering into metaphysics, report their visions in terms to be apprehended only by those who have toiled long in mastering the attenuated distinctions they insist upon with the aid of hybrid words, barbarously offensive in their composition; and what makes the matter worse is that these technical terms are often only written; they are rarely spoken; that is to say, they have not really become part of our English

146

speech; they are still imported aliens sometimes of mongrel ancestry.

Of course, this is no new thing; but it is
now and in English a thing of a more evil import than ever before. Our language is to-day
in danger of a dropsy. Our printed vocabulary
is swollen with unpronounced words, with words
which possibly appeal to the eye but which
hardly ever fall upon the ear. And the disease
is contagious, for if we are too frequently exposed to hybrid polysyllables, we may not be
able to resist them. What we need to fortify
ourselves with against insidious infection is a
tonic. We need to write as we speak,—and to
take care in speaking to use the simple and
more vigorous words of everyday life. We need
to cast out the fear of being considered unduly
colloquial. We need to forswear ink-horn terms
and to stick to the speech of the people,—as
Lincoln did. Milton does not hesitate to write
he *came off*, meaning he escaped; and Shakspere speaks of the fingers as *pickers and steal-
ers*. Shall we be afraid and ashamed to follow
in the footsteps of Milton and of Shakspere?

Especially is this warning necessary to the
poets, who have in the past half-century often
yielded to the charm of Tennyson's effeminate
felicities. Yet Tennyson himself could be ner-
vously masculine when he put forth his full

strength as he did in the splendid and sonorous stanzas of the 'Revenge.' Of late there are welcome signs that our lyrists are wearying of Latinizing. If the poetry of our language is about to recapture the colloquial daring of Shakspere and Milton and Tennyson (when this Victorian bard is most manly), then, so Dr. Henry Bradley tells us, this may be taken "as the surest sign of what we have often heard of—a poetic revival. If it is to get new values out of English . . . it will go for its technical substance to contemporary speech first and afterward to the great language of its old triumphs."

What the true poet yearns for is the uncontaminated word, the verbal coin unworn by incessant usage, the fresh flower of speech with the dew still on it. He relishes a term with a tang to it, with a savor and a flavor of its own, with sharpness of edge. If only he has the courage to use them he can find these words in our common speech; and it is his privilege to lift them up to his level and to ennoble them. It is in the pursuit of the unhackneyed word that the English poets of a hundred years ago returned to Chaucer (as Spenser had done two centuries earlier) and brought back to us not a few nouns and adjectives and verbs which were new because they were so old that they had been retired from service and forgotten. The language of poetry was enriched by this borrowing from the past, by this resuscitation of departed words restored to life by the magic wand of poetry.

III

WHILE our modern English has as its basis the local dialect of the Londoners, it began immediately to invite the aid of other contemporary dialects, Northern as well as Southern, taking at will whatever word or usage it found itself in need of. And this has been one of the means whereby it has been able to keep the judicious balance between the homely words of the plain people and the lordly words of the scholars. English has continually refreshed itself by drawing upon its own wells, fed by native springs and uncontaminated by the classics.

Long centuries ago a host of expressions which had at first fallen strangely on the ears of the Londoners, became in time familiar in their mouths,—just as there are locutions in modern Italian which are not Florentine, but Roman and even Neapolitan, and just as there are turns of phrase in Spanish which are not Castilian but Aragonese and even Catalan. When a dialect is lifted from its humble condition and becomes a national tongue, it is like the banyantree of the Orient,—from every far-extending branch it sends down tendrils which suck nourishment from the soil immediately beneath them and so serve to support the limbs from which they had hung dependent. *Uncouth*, for example, was taken into standard English from the dialect of the Scots; and *vat* and *vixen* are spellings and pronunciations from the dialect of Wessex. This method of strengthening our vocabulary has been utilized from a time "whereof the memory of man runneth not to the contrary"; and it is as useful now. As Skeat said, "we shall often do well to borrow from our dialects many terms that are still fresh and racy, and instinct with significance." It is a constant corrective of our latterday tendency to Latinize unduly.

It will be a sad and sorrowful day for the language and for those who love its sturdiness, when it ceases to seek support in the soil from which it sprang and when it renounces its precious privilege of replenishing its supply of words from its own hidden stores. Why should we call a new thing an *aeroplane* when we could more simply call it an *airplane?* Why should we term the operator of this machine an *aviator*, when we could as easily term him an *airman?* Why should we speak of the *aviation* service when we are free to speak of it as the *air* service?

Now and again, no doubt, it may be advisable, or even on occasion necessary, to compound a new name for a new thing from the Latin or the Greek; but we do this always at our peril. If we succumb to the temptation to call it by the horrific name of trinitrotoluol we need not be surprized when it speedily insists on styling itself T. N. T. which is not a word and not even the initials of three words.

In his memorable introduction to the second series of the 'Biglow Papers' Lowell told us that it had long seemed to him "that the great vice of American writing and speaking was a studied want of simplicity, that we were in danger of coming to look upon our mother-tongue as a dead language, to be sought in the grammar and dictionary rather than in the heart, and that our only chance of escape was by seeking it at its living sources among those who were, as Scottowe says of Major General Gibbons, 'divinely illiterate.' . . . It is only from its roots in the living generations of men that a language can be reinforced with fresh vigor for its needs; what may be called a literate dialect grows ever more and more pedantic, till it becomes at last as unfitting a vehicle for living thought as Monkish Latin. . . . True vigor and heartiness of phrase do not pass from page to page, but from man to man, where the brain is kindled and the lips suppled by down-right living interests and by passion in its very throe."

Later in the same paper Lowell expressed his relish for the homely picturesqueness of his native Yankee. He approved of our replevined verb, to *wilt*, expressing the first stage of wither-ing in a green plant. He held that "pure *cussedness*" was admirable "to vent certain con-temptuously indignant moods in a rough and ready way"; and he took pleasure in tracing it back to Chaucer. He was able also to locate *hot-foot*—"he followed them hot-foot,"—in the old French romance, 'Tristan'; and this vigor-ous vocable has recently been restored to new English romance by Kipling, who has a discerning eye for expressive words. Lowell also declared that another Yankee word was beautiful, *moon-glade,*—the track of moonlight on water; and we can only wonder that its beauty has not long ago tempted one or another of our native songsters.

Edward Fitzgerald, the translator of Omar Khayyam, amused himself by compiling sev-eral lists of East-Anglian words and phrases, some of which are not unfamiliar to Ameri-cans, *foot-loose* for one. Others deserve to be better known. *Sunway*—the path of the sun's rays over the sea—is a fit companion to *moon-*

glade. *Rimple* is an East-Anglian variant of
ripple,—the waves *rimpled.* But *brabble* is
perhaps the best of them,—the *brabble* of the
brook. How is it that Tennyson did not
make captive that toothsome word?

In Mrs. Wright's 'Rustic Speech and Folk-
Lore,' which rambles around in dialect after
dialect and which runs down a host of locutions used by the divinely illiterate, we find
feckless and *peart,* which do not fall strangely
on American ears. She rescues one horrific
word, *ugsome,* a powerful substitute for *fright-
ful* or *ghastly;* I seem to recall its use in some
forgotten tale of an Appalachian feud. But
fratch was entirely new to me; it serves to describe a noisy brawl. Mrs. Wright also points
out that *yonderly* is an excellent synonym for
"over there in the distance."

I do not doubt that even a hasty dip into the
word-lists from different sections of our own
country which have been printed in the journal
of the American Dialect Society would reward
the seeker after homely words deserving of
rescue. And some day, sooner or later, we
shall have an 'American Dialect Dictionary'
to companion the stately tomes of Wright's
'English Dialect Dictionary,' altho its editor
will have a more difficult task in sorting and
sifting than his British predecessor.

IV

It has been the object of this brief inquiry not to single out a host of dialect words demanding recognition, but to call attention to dialect in general as a storehouse of terms, often picturesque and generally expressive, from which the language of literature might be invigorated. We need to see the peril in our tendency to Latinize and to be on our guard against the temptation to agree with the London alderman who objected to the final phrase of Canning's fine epitaph on Pitt, "He died poor," proposing as a substitute, "He expired in indigent circumstances." And we must also cultivate a liking for the homely phrase which smacks of the soil.

The two sisters of a friend of mine, staying at a summer hotel on the New England coast, once went on a walk and lost their way. They met an old farmer who had a kindly smile and they asked him for guidance. "Do you want the nighest way or the sightliest?" was his reply to their inquiry. They smiled back at him and said that they would rather go home by the sightliest way. "Well," he explained with a grave face but with a twinkle in his eye, "that *is* the nighest!"

(1919.)

154

VIII

A CONFUSION OF TONGUES

VIII

A CONFUSION OF TONGUES

I

IN the final years of the last century, when
the people of the United States were moved
at last to go to the rescue of the people of Cuba,
there were not wanting friends of Spain in
the other Latin countries, who were convinced
that the result of the conflict would be certain
defeat of our army by the better disciplined and
better trained troops of our foe. As one perfervid enthusiast expressed it, there could be no
doubt that "the pure-blooded soldiers of Spain
would win an easy victory over the mongrel
hordes of America." The wish was father to
the thought; but perhaps the discourteous expression was due in part to a fear that the result of the war might not be what the speaker
hoped.

That the description of the American forces
as "mongrel hordes" was intended to be offensive, admits of no doubt. And yet however distasteful the words may be to us, they
are not altogether inexact. The inhabitants

157

of the United States are a mixed race; they are descended from ancestors of many stocks; they have not been completely fused together in the melting-pot; they have not yet attained to the racial unity of the French, for example, or of the Danes; and therefore those who think they have cause for disliking us have a warrant of a sort for calling us a mongrel horde. But no warrant can be found by anybody for crediting the Spanish soldiers with purity of blood. In the course of the centuries the original inhabitants of Spain, whoever they may have been, have had to mingle their blood with Phœnicians and Greeks, with Carthaginians and Romans, with Goths and Vandals, with Moors and Arabs, until the Spaniards are perhaps better entitled to be termed mongrels than any other people in Europe and more especially than the English, who had by Shakspere's time absorbed and assimilated Celts and Romans, Danes and Saxons, Normans and Flemings. Even if any stone is good enough to throw at a dog, there is no propriety in one mongrel throwing stones at another.

What happened centuries ago in the British Isles and in the Iberian peninsula is still happening in the United States; and it bids fair to continue for two or three score years longer, if not for two or three hundred. The successive invaders of Great Britain were most of them scions of the same stock; but the races that overran Spain one after another were as different ethnically as the later immigrants to America are from the earlier Pilgrims and Cavaliers. Truly we are now a diversity of creatures; and yet we are imposing the dominant Anglo-Saxon ideals of liberty under the law upon men and women who do not care greatly for liberty and who have little reverence for law. And in so doing we have to depend mainly upon the unifying power of the English language.

So long as our immigrants came to us from Northern Europe, from the British Isles, from Scandinavia and from Germany, they could be absorbed in the course of time as readily as their kindred had been assimilated in Great Britain centuries ago; but the process does not work as swiftly or as satisfactorily now that they are coming from Southern and from Eastern Europe and even from Asia Minor. Those who emigrated from these remoter regions in the opening years of this century, are truly "mongrel hordes"; and the difficulty of making them into Americans is indisputable. This difficulty would be increased if we were still welcoming new comers of races ethnically unrelated to ours, the Japanese, for one, and the Chinese, for another.

Once upon a time the conversation of a little
knot of artists, gathered in a cozy corner of a
New York club, happened to turn on a man,
who had a Japanese woman for a mother and
a German Hebrew for a father, and who was
an American citizen, speaking and writing
English. One of the group put the question
as to what race this man of commingled ancestry really belonged to; and the wit of the
club promptly found the answer. "Of course he
is a Mongrelian!"

II

THIS smart saying returned to the memory
of another member of the group, a little later,
when he chanced to be passing thru one of the
several Italian quarters of New York and when
his eyes lighted upon a sign which declared the
little shop beneath it to be a *grossaria*. He
had enough Italian to know that *epiceria* was
the proper word; and he guessed at once that
the owner of the grocery store had Italianized
the word in use among Americans. (The British,
oddly enough, are in the habit of calling such a
shop an "Italian warehouse," perhaps because
it has for sale olive oil and macaroni and sar-
dines.) Here, he said to himself, is a specimen
of the dialect of the Mongrelians; and he was
led to inquire if this was a solitary instance of

the influence exerted by our language upon the vocabulary of the Italian immigrants, surrounded on all sides by users of English.

Once started upon this quest he soon discovered that *grossaria* was only one of dozens and scores, and perhaps hundreds of words Italianate in form but English in fact. He learned that the Italian *padrone*, almost the exact equivalent of our American *boss*, was yielding to *bosso*. He found *cocco* for *cook*, *carro* for *car*, *coppo* for *policeman* (cop), *cotto* for *coat*, *giobba* for *job*, *bucco-taimo* for *time-book*, *moni* for *money*, *trobolo* for *trouble*, *visco* for *whiskey*, and *storo* for *store*,—all of them seemingly Italian, all of them familiar to and frequently used by the Italians of New York, and all of them absolutely incomprehensible to the Italians of Rome and Naples and Venice. He was informed by Professor Livingston that this infiltration of English into Italian had not affected as many verbs as nouns, altho even here it could be seen at work, as in *bordare* for *to board*, *ingaggiare* for *to engage*, *strappare* for *to strop* (a razor), *sbluffo* for *to bluff*, and *godaella* for *to discharge*, —this last being obviously made out of "go to hell," which plainly implies that the act of hiring and firing is not always done with the courtesy customary to the Italians themselves.

But the nouns are at once more numerous and

161

more picturesque; and it would be impossible not to call attention to *besinisso* for *business*, *muffo-piccio* for *moving-pictures*, and more particularly to *carpentiere* for *carpenter* and *briccoliere* for *bricklayer!* Also not to be omitted are *orraite* for *all right*, *barratende* for *bar-tender*, *richermanne* for *rich man*, *grollo* for *growler* (a can of beer), and *grignolo* for *greenhorn*.

This investigation once entered upon, the earnest inquirer was moved to ask whether a similar influence was being exerted upon German and upon French as these languages are spoken by the New York immigrants from one or the other side of the Rhine. And he was rewarded by hearing of a German compositor in a ramshackle printing office who complained that the window *arbeitet nicht*, and asking the owner of the shop if it could not be *fixirt*, and of a German cobbler who asked if the shoes brought for repair were to be both *gesohlt* and *gehielt*.

He was regaled by the story of a Frenchman, who interrupted a street row between two of his compatriots with the inquiry: "*Quel est la matière?*"—a question which the two score members of the French Academy would have puzzled over in vain. Apparently French has suffered far less than Italian, perhaps because the immigrants from France are less likely to herd together, and also because they are more likely to have the rudiments of education than the immigrants from Italy. Still it is not at all uncommon to hear Frenchmen in New York speak of *bisenesse*, where the Frenchmen of Paris would speak of *les affaires*. They have been known also to call a *street-car* a *char*, and to use the Americanism *block* for a *street-block*. They sometimes speak of the *elevated railroad* as the *élevé*, and of the *ferry* as the *ferri*. And a friend from Canada supplied the information that the more or less intimate association of the French-speaking Canadians with the English-speaking Canadians had emboldened the former to say "Je vais *walker*," and to describe a fault-finding woman as "trop *kickeuse*."

III

As like causes are certain to produce like effects, we need not doubt that a corresponding influence is now being exerted by the surrounding Spanish language upon the speech of the hundreds of thousands of Italian immigrants in the Argentine, and also that it was exerted upon Spanish itself long ago during the many years when Naples was ruled by Madrid. So a similar impression is made upon the vocabulary of the members of the American colony in Paris, who are led by insensible steps to import into their vocabulary not a few French words in meanings wholly unknown to the residents of London and New York. Perhaps it is due to this persistent group of denationalized Americans, who have failed to make themselves at home in France, despite long domicile, that we are all now getting accustomed more or less to the use of to *assist* at a concert, when we have merely been present at it.

Huxley once quoted from Buffon the assertion that "to understand what has happened, and even what will happen, we have only to examine what is happening." This is true in linguistics as it is in natural science. The effect of the impinging of an encircling speech upon the vocabulary of a smaller group is visible here in New York now as it must have been visible in Naples once upon a time, as it was certainly visible in England after the Norman came over. And it is one of the causes which combined to bring about the English language of to-day, mainly Teutonic in its structure and yet largely Gallic in its vocabulary.

English has never relinquished its ancient prerogative of taking over foreign words and phrases, even when it did not need them, any more than Italian, having *epiciria* and *padrone*, needed *grossaria* and *bosso*. Indeed, English has often cast out a perfectly good word of its

164

own to borrow a foreign word, no better fitted for service. When it has done so, it has some-times repented and reversed its action, reviving the dead and gone native term. Dr. Henry Bradley has told us that writers of English in the thirteenth and fourteenth centuries felt themselves at liberty to use French words at will, making them English at least for the moment. But as these words were only tem-porarily useful they fell out of fashion, sooner or later, so that "many which supplied no per-manent need of the language have long been obsolete." There were, indeed, so many of these imported terms that the students of lan-guage have had to devise a specific name for them; they are called "loan words," being bor-rowed only for a brief period and in the end relinquished to their original owner. They may be likened to the host of Italian laborers who come over to work in America for a few years only and who return sooner or later to their native land, having perhaps taken out their first papers, without persisting in their effort to acquire American citizenship.

It is idle to speculate as to the possible results of an impossible event. Yet there is a certain fascination in asking ourselves to consider the effect upon the future of the Italian language if a total destruction of Italy should occur, by an earthquake or some other appalling convulsion of nature. If all the inhabitants of the storied peninsula were to be suddenly annihilated, leaving alive to speak its soft and liquid speech only their expatriated countrymen in North and South America, the language ennobled by the Four Poets might cease to be; it might survive only in its mighty literature; it might split into two diverging tongues, one of them profoundly modified by the English of the Yankees and the other transformed in another direction by the Spanish of the Argentines, the Yanquis of the South.

The divergence would be accelerated by the fact that the immense mass of the Italian immigrants into the two Americas are relatively illiterate, and would therefore be released from loyalty to the literature of the past. Each of the separated hordes would be subdued to what it worked in; and the result would be two new forms of Italian, probably as different as Portuguese is from Spanish, and more different than peasant Norwegian is from peasant Danish.

But neither of these two resulting languages, even if it ceased to be Tuscan, could fairly be denounced as a Mongrelian tongue. That indignity it would be spared.

(1919.)

166

IX

LEARNING A LANGUAGE

IX

LEARNING A LANGUAGE

I

ONE of the most obvious results of our entry into the war was to attract our attention to the fact that many American citizens, who were called to the colors, did not speak English and did not understand it sufficiently to learn the manual of the arms. And an equally obvious result of the transportation of our army to France was the discovery that very few of our soldiers had even an elementary knowledge of the French language. Peace has brought with it alluring possibilities of widely increased foreign trade, especially with Latin America, and we are told that we are handicapped by our lack of competent men able to speak, to read, and to write Spanish or Portuguese, without which it is impossible to establish satisfactory business relations with the friendly foreigners to the south of us.

At the Paris Conference it was a disadvantage to President Wilson and to Mr. Lloyd George that neither of them was conversant with

French, whereas M. Clemenceau undoubtedly profited by his knowledge of English, due to his protracted sojourn in the United States, many years ago. French is still the official language of diplomacy; and it has long been the necessary second language of educated men whatever their native tongue. In the last half-century, however, owing to the constant expansion of the British Commonwealth and to the steady growth of the United States, English has been acquired by an ever-increasing number of Italians and Spaniards, French and Germans; and it is rapidly taking a place alongside French. Indeed, we might almost assert that English now stands an alternative of French as the indispensable second language. At the meetings of one of the subsidiary committees of the Paris Conference, the proceedings were at first conducted in French, only to be continued in English when it was discovered that more than a half of the members could speak our tongue, while less than half of them were able to use the language of the city in which they were sitting.

It is true that Americans are only a little more unlikely to have acquired any foreign speech than are the British or the French. Our most important customer is the British Empire; and the United States is its most important customer. The French have so long cherished the belief that they are the intellectual leaders of the world that they have until recently shown comparatively little desire for foreign travel, and therefore they have felt little need of mastering any language but their own. It is in the smaller countries that the acquisition of foreign tongues is imperative. Switzerland, for example, has a mixed population, partly French, partly German, and partly Italian; and the Swiss schools are practically compelled to pay special attention to the teaching of languages. So it is that a Swiss, even when he is not a man of cosmopolitan culture, is likely to speak both French and German, and not unlikely also to speak English, which is certain to be useful to him, now that Switzerland has become the playground of Europe, filled with Americans and British, especially in the summer, but increasingly in the winter also. In Holland, which is a center of international trade and of international travel, the signs in the railroad stations are in four languages, Dutch, German, French, and English; and almost every Hollander of any education is master of French and English.

To this study of foreign languages the Swiss and the Dutch are impelled by two circumstances, the medley of speech among their own citizens, and the pressure of their immediate neighbors. Neither of these circumstances exerts any influence upon us here in the United States. Our neighbor to the north shares English with us; and our relations with our neighbor to the south have never been intimate enough, or pressing enough, to make us feel the necessity of preparing ourselves to talk to him in his own tongue. And altho we also have unassimilated foreign elements in our population, we have always proceeded on the assumption that the assimilation was certain to take place sooner or later. We have not doubted that immediate and incessant contact with those of us who spoke only English would force the immigrant to familiarize himself with our speech, and even in time to renounce his native tongue and to employ English, not only in his business affairs, but also in the privacy of his own family. The war has revealed to us that in this expectation we have been too optimistic, and that we have been too tolerant of the many oases of foreign speech, continuing alien even after several generations of existence in America.

Measures have already been taken to remedy the unsatisfactory conditions laid bare in "the drugged and doubting years"; and we have now no doubt that the first and most essential evidence of the Americanization of the citizens who have come to us from abroad is their ability to use our language. Yet our success in inducing the immigrant to speak English and even to think in English, while it was not so complete as we were accustomed to believe, was still very remarkable. Countless thousands of men and women from all parts of the world, have abandoned their native tongues and have become accustomed to the use of our language. Their children have gone to the public schools, and year by year these young people have been exerting an irresistible pressure upon their parents. The elders might ardently desire not to abandon their foreign ways of thinking, and to preserve their birthright of usage and tradition; but the youngsters did not need to make any effort to renounce these usages and these traditions in so far as they were discordant with American ideals; they simply shed this ancestral heritage to rid themselves of every importation which might tend to prevent their acceptance as Americans, and as Americans only.

Our reason for a growing familiarity with our vocabulary to be noted in foreigners abroad is that English is the language of the out-door sports which have been assiduously cultivated of late all over the world. Cricket may still belong only to the British, and baseball may still be our own exclusive possession; but lawn-tennis and golf, racing and yachting are now popular among many peoples. Thousands of sportsmen who know no other English, freely talk about *dead heats* and *jockeys*, about *handicaps* and *matches*. I recall that on my last visit to the Engadine, some twenty summers ago, I found a very cosmopolitan crowd, composed of Russians and Austrians, Italians and French, with a slight sprinkling of Americans and English; and as I passed the nets of the tennis courts I could hear *Ready* and *Play* not unduly disguised by alien accents.

That English is the language most necessary to a man engaged in international trade is indisputable; and that the literature of our language is as alluring as the literature of the French tongue is equally undeniable. In fact, the unrivalled number of possible readers for a book written in English has tempted several alien authors to abandon their native tongues and to compose their works in our more widely distributed language. The late Marten Martens forswore the speech of his fellow Hollanders, to write in the speech of the peoples of Great Britain and the United States; and the living Joseph Conrad is an example of the power of a Pole to master the secret of nervous and sinewy English. Nevertheless, other literatures have a potent appeal; and we need to do busi-

174

ness with other peoples than our kin across the Atlantic and across the St. Lawrence. Therefore we may hope that the desire to acquire a foreign tongue, made manifest in many ways since the cessation of the war, will bear abundant fruit.

II

STRANGE as it may seem, one of the most marked advantages of English as a language is likely to be found a temporary obstacle to the learning of another tongue by those to whom English is native. More than forty years ago Richard Grant White made bold to describe ours as a grammarless tongue. Of course, this was an overstatement of the case; but it was not exactly a misstatement. Compared with German or with Greek, English is immeasurably simpler in its syntax; and it has less grammatical machinery than French or Italian.

In the first place, our genders are natural, whereas the genders in almost every other language are artificial and arbitrary. In German the moon is masculine, *der Mond*, and the sun is feminine, *die Sonne;* and in French the moon is feminine, *la lune*, and the sun is masculine, *le soleil*. What is even more absurd in our eyes is that in German a maiden is neuter, *das Mädchen*. In English, nouns implying sex are '

175

either masculine or feminine; and all sexless objects are neuter. It is true that we may say when we see a yacht ballooning out its canvas as it rounds the stake-boat: "Isn't *she* a beauty?" But this is only a casual lapse into poetry; and when we are talking prose, when we are buying or selling a yacht, we speak of the boat as *it*.

In the second place we have no enforced agreements; for example, the article *the* does not change with the gender or the number of the noun to which it is affixed. Nor does the adjective, which may precede it, vary in gender and number in conformity with the gender and number of the noun. We say *the white man* and *the white women*, whereas the French have to say *l'homme blanc* and *les femmes blanches*.

Not only are our articles and adjectives subject to no variation, but our nouns also do not change their terminations to indicate their several cases. Where we say *of the muses* the Latins said *musarum*. We construct our cases by the use of a few prepositions, and as a result of this bold improvement in linguistic method our nouns are not required to wag their tails, so to speak. And as it is with our nouns, so it is with our verbs, or at least with the immense majority of them, with those which we regard as "regular." We make the past tense by

adding a *d* or an *ed*, *I love* and *I loved;* but we
make the future and the conditional by prefixing an auxiliary, *"I shall love,"* or *"I should
love,"* whereas the French *I love* is *j'aime, I loved*
is *j'amai* or *j'aimais, I shall love* is *j'aimerai*, and
I should love is *j'aimerais*. That is to say, in
other languages the verb makes its changes of
tense by modifications of the end of the word,
and the verb in English makes most of its changes
by prefixing auxiliaries, leaving the word itself
unchanged.

This simplification of grammatical structure
has endowed modern English with an energy
and an immediate efficiency possessed by no
other language, ancient or modern. Possibly
this large gain has been accompanied by some
slight loss; and there may be subtle and delicate
shades of meaning not so easily conveyed in
English as they were in Greek, with its complexity of declensions, agreements, and conjugations. The more primitive a language is the
more intricate is it in its grammar; and Anglo-
Saxon, the remote ancestor of our tongue, was
encumbered with a complexity of syntactical
devices, which were rudely brushed off by the
collision with Norman French in the centuries
which followed the Conquest. It is because
we have scrapped most of our conjugations,
nearly all of our declensions and agreements,

and all of our artificial genders, that the Danish philologist, Jespersen, felt at liberty to call English the most advanced of modern languages, the least cumbrous grammatically, the simplest and most logical in its directness.

As it is possible to teach formal grammar in English only by arbitrarily lending to our speech the grammatical framework of another tongue, Latin for example, the teaching of formal grammar has gone out of fashion; and therefore the average American who begins the study of any other language, ancient or modern, has first of all to familiarize himself with what seems to him an unnatural way of expression, the necessity of which he has never had occasion to suspect. Here is where even a smattering of Latin, a term or two of school work in a dead language, proves itself of service to the student starting in on French or Spanish; and an acquaintance with Latin, however slight, makes much easier the acquisition of the vocabulary of the modern languages directly descended from the speech of the Romans—French and Italian, Spanish and Portuguese.

The instruction given in the elementary courses in foreign languages is generally founded on the theory that the student desires to master the tongue he is undertaking to learn, that he wishes to know it thoroly, that he wants to be able to speak it, to read it, and to write it, that he is looking forward to the secure enjoyment of its literature, present and past. Courses so planned are satisfactory for students who have these intentions and who expect to be able to devote the time and the energy needful to possess the foreign language as completely as may be. Yet these courses are not so satisfactory to the many students who are more or less in a hurry, who need the foreign tongue for present use and for a special purpose.

A classical scholar, for example, may want to be able to read the German introductions and annotations of Greek and Latin texts, without any impulse to learn how to speak German; and a traveler, who cares little for literature and who never expects to read Molière, and still less Rabelais, but who is going to Paris and wishes to be able to order his dinner and to direct his taxi-driver, is ready to content himself with a fair command of contemporary colloquial French, very different in its texture from the stately French of Corneille and Racine. What this traveler needs is the faculty of speaking French sufficiently to be able to get around in Paris; he does not need to know how to write it, and scarcely needs to know how to read it. Indeed, to such a prospective traveler there will be immediate profit in learning entirely by ear, by word of mouth, and without looking at the printed page where his eye would find words so spelled as to make their pronunciation more difficult. After he has gained a certain facility in speaking, it will be just so much easier for him to take up a French newspaper and to puzzle out its contents.

III

THERE is a vital fact often overlooked by the formulators of comprehensive courses; and this is that we need only a sharply restricted vocabulary to carry on the ordinary business of life. A few hundred words are sufficient; and even in our own tongue few of us use more. It is this restricted vocabulary that the beginner ought to master as speedily as possible; and he ought to begin to use his few hundred words at once. Fifty years ago when the people of the United States had accustomed themselves to paper money, greenbacks, and shin-plasters, and when "Old Bill Allen" of Ohio was asserting that the resumption of specie payments was "a barren ideality," another statesman declared that "the way to resume is to resume." The way to learn to speak French or Spanish or Italian is to speak it, to speak it in season and out, to accustom the tongue and the ear to it.

Of course, the beginner will make blunders,

and many of them; and some of them will be ridiculous. None the less must he persevere, seeking out every opportunity to practise. He will find that foreigners in general are more polite than we are. They may have to conceal a smile at his misfit sentences; but they are not likely to laugh out and they are likely to be encouraging. And it is with those who have the desired language as a native tongue that the beginner ought to converse as often as possible, never with his fellow learners who will be far less considerate and far less courteous than the foreigners. I know a man who speaks French fluently, but not accurately, and who never hesitates to drop into conversation with Frenchmen, while he is always cautious in airing his French before less tolerant Americans. Frenchmen do not expect any American to be accurate in his use of their delicately organized language, whereas Americans, with their memories full of rules recently got by heart, are prone to be unsympathetic listeners. In France itself the traveler finds that the natives are swift to compliment him on his French—especially if they are trying to sell him something.

It may be pointed out also that in speaking his native tongue every man uses what has here been termed the restricted vocabulary of everyday life, and in addition to this he uses the special vocabulary of his own calling, rich in technical terms of exact meaning, familiar to him and yet not known, or only a little known, to men of other trades and professions. The printers have their own vocabulary, so have the physicians, so have the railroad men. Now, from out all the countless thousands of words in a foreign language, the beginner needs to possess himself, first of all, of the restricted vocabulary of everyday life, and then, as soon as may be, of the special vocabulary of the art or science in which he is most interested.

If he is merely a traveler he must set himself to understand and to employ the terms of the railroad, the hotel, the restaurant, and the theater. If she is a woman of fashion she will find profit in acquiring the words and phrases she will have occasion to use at the jeweler's, the dress-maker's, the milliner's, and the department-stores. It is hopeless for the average American to expect to make himself really familiar with the whole of a foreign language abounding in special vocabularies which have no immediate value for him. But it is really not difficult for him to familiarize himself with those portions of the desired tongue for which he has the most pressing need.

On his return from his hunting trip in the interior of Africa, Theodore Roosevelt was in-

vited to the capitals of Europe and was enter-
tained by kings and queens. He has recorded
that he found most of these monarchs able to
hold converse with him in his own tongue.
When they did not speak English they talked
with him in French. "I am sorry to say," he
confessed, "that I am too much like Chaucer's
Abbess, in that my French is more like that of
Stratford-at-Bow than the French of Paris.
But still, such as it is, I speak it with daring
fluency." This was an example of Roosevelt's
characteristic common sense. His French might
not be impeccable, but such as it was it served
his purpose. "Daring fluency" is exactly what
every beginner ought to strive for.

When the beginner wishes to learn to read
rather than to speak the foreign language, he
will do well to acquaint himself first of all with
its formal grammatical framework, with its
conjugations and declensions and agreements.
When this acquaintance with the structure has
been acquired, he ought at once to start in reading as much as he can; and he will find it profit-
able to begin with the newspaper, because he
will already have a certain familiarity with the
subject-matter, which will help him to guess at
the drift of the sentences and the paragraphs.
In New York, for example, there is a good French
daily, the *Courier des Etats Unis*, a good Italian

daily, the *Eco d'Italia*, and a good Spanish daily, the *Prensa*. In default of an easily accessible daily, an illustrated weekly will serve the same purpose; and its pictures will help to elucidate the text. He will need a dictionary, of course; but he ought not to go to it too often. It is better to get into the habit of guessing at the meaning and of taking in the purport of the sentence as a whole. He will often misread; but he will be surprized to find how soon words and phrases begin to stick in his memory.

When he has made a sufficient progress with the newspaper, he may supplement it with plays, preferably in one act, so as to shorten the effort. If the plays chosen are modern, the student will be getting an insight into colloquial speech, which is certain to be of service to him whenever he decides that he also wishes to learn how to speak the foreign tongue. Plays are better fitted for the beginner than novels, since they are wholly in dialogue and devoid of the descriptions and analyses which are far less easy to interpret. In time he may go on to novels, and, if need be, to the technical treatises on his own special subject.

The experimental psychologists have discovered of late that men and women may be divided roughly into two groups. In one group are those who are most easily approached thru the eye and in the other those who are most easily approached thru the ear. The first are visualizers and the second are auditors. Some of us are bored and let our attention wander while we are listening to a lecture, altho we might read that lecture with interest and with appreciation if we found it in a book or a magazine. Others of us would not be attracted to the printed page while eagerly apprehending and retaining the thoughts as they fell from the lips of the speaker. Now, the visualizers will find it easier to learn to read a foreign language than to speak it; and the auditors will find it easier to learn to speak it than to read it. This is not to say that most of us lack the power to acquire a foreign tongue so that we can both read and speak it; it is only to point out which is the more advantageous way to begin the study. Of course, visualizers can acquire facility in speaking a foreign tongue and auditors in reading it; but it would be well for the members of the two groups to direct their earliest efforts along the line of least resistance.

(1920.)

X

THE ADVERTIZER'S ARTFUL AID

X

THE ADVERTIZER'S ARTFUL AID

I

THE incessant expansion of the vocabulary of English is due primarily of course to the essential energy of the Anglo-Saxon stock, to its persistent voyaging, to its prolific inventiveness, and to its daring imagination. A people always makes its language in its own image, and the English language is as vigorous, as impatient, as unpedantic and as illogical as are the two mighty peoples who hold it in common as a precious heritage. As these two peoples have multiplied more rapidly than any other, so their language has constantly increased its resources, until English has now a vocabulary ampler than that of any of its rivals. As there is not yet apparent any sign of the relaxing of this essential energy in the far-flung British Commonwealth or in these United States, there is no likelihood that the English language will surrender its right to make new words for new needs and to take over from foreign tongues any terms which it thinks it can use to advantage.

Exploration and colonization, invention and discovery, the advance of pure science and of applied science, progress in the fine arts and experiment in literature—these are all of them and each of them responsible for their several shares in the unending increase in the vocabulary of our English speech. But there has been at work of late—that is to say, in the past score of years, in the first two decades of the twentieth century—another impetus, the full effects of which are not yet visible. In fact, this new source of new words has never been accorded the recognition it deserves and demands. We have had our attention called to words of warfare with which we have had to store our memories in the long years of fighting, *slacker* and *tank*, *cooty* and *combing out*—vigorous words, born in the trenches and evolved by spontaneous generation; they are none the worse for their lowly origin, and in fact they owe to it their soldierly directness and swiftness.

Yet peace has her verbal victories no less than war; indeed, her linguistic conquests are more varied and of a more permanent utility. These peaceful words are made anywhere and everywhere. They are made while you wait, on the spur of the moment, at haphazard; they may be well-made or ill-made; and they must push their way speedily into general use or they will die an early death from inanition. There is, however, one manufactory of new words where the utmost care is taken to put together vocables which are reasonably certain to arrest attention and to win approval. A verbal factory of this sort is situated in almost every one of the advertizing agencies, which are now so widely scattered thruout the United States. The words these advertizers make are not often taken over from any other language, dead or alive; they are compounded to order, with the utmost caution and with an uncanny skill. They are put together with the hope that they will cling to the memory of those who read them for the first time; and the more completely this hope is justified, the more successful is the new label for a new thing.

We are now so thoroly accustomed to the exploits of the advertizer that we take them as a matter of course, rarely pausing to appreciate the art, or at least, the artfulness with which he has lured us into acceptance of the new name that he has manufactured for the new article he has been engaged to call to our attention. Nor is his inventive ingenuity confined to the creation of new words only; it extends even to the imaginative incarnation of non-existent persons. With some of these shadowy individuals, resident only in reiterated and constantly varied advertizements, we are as friendly as we are with the well-known characters in fiction; they are familiar in our mouths as household words; and we follow their adventures with unfailing and unflagging interest. It would never surprize us to learn that Sunny Jim had long ago made a runaway match with Phœbe Snow; that the offspring of this secret union, after "blacking up," had won fame on their own account as the Golddust Twins; and that the whole family had settled at last in Spotless Town.

So forcibly have these personalities impressed themselves upon our attention that we do not necessarily associate them with the specific wares which they sprang into being to advertize; and in so far as this is the case, we cannot but fear that their creators may have overshot the mark. This is, however, a mishap which the adroit artist in advertizing is generally able to avoid. We are in no danger of separating the word *kodak* from the photographic apparatus it designates; indeed, we are more likely to accept this specific word as a generic term large enough in its application to include all the rival cameras of a similar portability. We may almost assert that *kodak* is winning acceptance as a word in good standing in English, even if it also serves as the trademark of the manufacturer whose product it identifies. It has already passed from English into French and into German; and the globe-trotting American is able to purchase a kodak and any of its kodakcessories almost anywhere in the world.

II

WHAT should have been prefixed to this rambling disquisition is a copy of verses which I found in the flotsam and jetsam of journalism, credited only to a nameless exchange. I do not know therefore where it originally appeared or to whom the honor of its authorship should be ascribed. It may have been the product of the pen of that ubiquitous Mr. Anon, who is perhaps the most constant of contributors to unidentified exchanges. It was simply and boldly entitled "Ode"; and, as will be seen, it had a full Horatian flavor. Read aloud, with due emphasis and with proper respect for its lordly rhythm, it is undeniably possessed of a sonorous dignity. Perhaps there would be excess of praise if the suggestion were ventured that it sounded a little as if Horace himself had composed it, in some lost language of the past, possibly Etruscan, undecipherable until some patient explorer shall discover its Rosetta Stone. The fourth line, for example,

Postum nabisco,

has the very cadence of Horace's

Fusce pharetra.

193

ODE!

Chipeco thermos dioxygen, temco sonora tuxedo
Resinol fiat bacardi, camera ansco wheatena;
Antiskid pebeco calox, oleo tyco barometer
   Postum nabisco!

Prestolite arco congoleum, karo aluminum kryptok,
Crisco balopticon lysol, jello bellans, carborundum!
Ampico clysmic swoboda, pantasote necco britannica
   Encyclopedia?

When we undertake to analyze the vocabulary of this delectable specimen of neo-classic versification, we discover that less than a dozen of its words are recorded in the dictionaries of English: *aluminum, barometer, Britannica, camera, carborundum, dioxygen, encyclopedia* and *tuxedo.* Two of these may be only doubtfully English, since *carborundum*—superbly suggestive of the oretund Latin gerund—is the name given by its American inventor to a product so useful that it is exported to manufacturers thruout the world; and *tuxedo* is the name generally bestowed by Americans on the article of apparel which the British prefer to call a *dinner-jacket.* With the exception of *fiat*, the name of an Italian motor-car, made by the Fabbrica Italiano Automobili Torino, all the other words are to be credited to the ingenuity of the American advertizer; and at least one half of them, familiar as they may be to us on this side of the Western Ocean, are not yet known to our kin across the sea.

To identify the majority of these trademarks would be an excellent test of observation and of memory. First of all, we may single out a group of words artfully compounded to designate novelties of food and drink: *clysmic, crisco, jello, karo, nabisco, necco, postum,* and *wheatena.* And it is with surprize that we note the absence of *uneeda,* which we were justified in expecting to find here in company with its fellows, many of them less indelibly imprinted on our memories. Of most of these words the origin is not a little obscure, altho we perceive that *postum* perpetuates the name of its maker, and that *nabisco* is a foreshortening of National Biscuit Company. *Jello* is plainly intended to suggest *jelly.*

Second, we descry a group of words put together to provide names for articles of the toilet and of the household: *ampico, ansco, balopticon, calox, congoleum, lysol, kryptok, oleo, pebeco, resinol, sonora,* and *thermos.* Here again we miss *kodak* and *sapolio,* perhaps because they failed to fit into the meter. When we seek the materials out of which these words have been made, we cannot blunder if we decide that *oleo* harks back to the Latin, and *thermos* to the

Greek; and we can surmise that *ampico* is a summary telescoping of American Piano Company.

Third, and less numerous, is the group of names for patented and protected accessories of the automobile: *antiskid, pantasote*, and *prestolite*, a group far smaller than we should have expected to find in the prevailing effulgence of automobile advertizing.

As for the remainder of these hand-made words, I must confess that I am at a loss to suggest any satisfactory classification. Indeed, I do not identify all of them, altho there are none with which I feel myself absolutely unfamiliar. I believe, however, that *swoboda* is a name belonging to or assumed by an exponent of physical culture, and intended to designate the specific exercises which he recommends. One or another of the rest of these more or less felicitous examples of trade nomenclature may have been made up to individualize an edible or a potable, a toilet preparation or an automobile accessory, a camera or a player-piano. Their origin may be abandoned to the researches of linguistic investigators more patient and more persevering than I am.

I have already noted that nearly all the artificial vocables, whose dexterous collocation lends to this Horatian ode its ample sonority, are of domestic manufacture. Only a very few of them would evoke recognition from an Englishman; and what a Frenchmen or a German would make out of the eight lines, it is beyond human power even to conjecture. Corresponding words have been devised in France and in Germany, but only infrequently; and apparently the invention of trademark names is not a customary procedure on the part of foreign advertizers. The British, altho less affluent in this respect than we are, seem to be a little more inclined to employ the device than their competitors on the Continent. Every American, traveling on the railways which converge upon London, must have experienced a difficulty in discovering whether the station at which his train has paused is Stoke Pogis or Bovril, Chipping Norton or Mazzawattee. None the less is it safe to say that the concoction of a similar ode by the aid of the trademark words invented in the British Isles would be a task of great difficulty on account of the paucity of terms sufficiently artificial to bestow the exotic remoteness which is accountable for the fragrant aroma of the American ode.

III

MANY of the incessant accretions to our constantly expanding speech have been the result of happy accidents and have slipped into general circulation without comment or resistance. They may have been derived from the place where the thing they describe originated, like *currants* (from Corinth), and *cambric* (from Cambrai). They may have kept the name of the originator of the object they designate, like *sandwich* and *gatling*, or they may preserve the name of the first user of the article, like *cardigan* and *sontag*. But the new words devised by the advertizing agents are not accidental or fortuitous in their genesis; they are the result of volition; and the maker of each of them knew what he was doing and did it with malice prepense. *Balopticon* and *kryptok*, for instance, do not fall as trippingly upon the ear, and therefore do not as readily affix themselves to the memory as do *kodak* and *crisco*, *uneeda* and *calox*.

As poetry ought to be simple, sensuous and passionate, so an artistically compounded trademark word ought to be simple, euphonious and emphatic; and perhaps emphasis is the most necessary of these three qualities. The advertizers have mastered one of the secrets of per-

suasion; they are unhesitatingly bold in assertion; but they are not too bold. They seek
rather to coax or cajole us than to command
and compel us to purchase the wares they are
vending. More often than not there is a sweet
reasonableness in their appeal; their attitude is
altruistic rather than selfish; they are advising
us for our own good. They intimate that if we
are wise we will heed their monitions and let
ourselves be guided by their counsel. Their
modest frankness is engaging; and it inclines
us to believe in their honesty.

This, indeed, is one of the advantages of the
more recent development of the advertizing art:
it makes for honesty. It pays to advertize—
but only when the object advertized is good of
its kind and reasonable in its price. It does
not pay to push an article with which the pur-
chaser will be disappointed. The buyer must
get his money's worth; he must be satisfied with
his bargain and more than satisfied or he will
not repeat his purchase. The aim of the advertizer is to create a habit. The plausible advertizement can make only the first sale; and
the subsequent sales on which the maker relies
for his profit depend on the value of the article
itself. You cannot fool all the people all the
time, and it is safe to say that anything which
has been widely advertized for a succession of

years must have merit, even if it may not be all that is claimed for it.

In most cases, however, the advertizer is careful not to overstate his case; rather does he understate it. Not for him are the flamboyant alliterations and the polychrome adjectives of a three-ringed circus. He shrinks from excessive self-exhibition; in fact, he seeks to be unobtrusive, strange as this suggestion may seem. He tries to focus the attention of the possible purchasers on his clear and simple statement of the merits of the article he is vaunting without forcing them to observe the constructive skill with which his statement has been made. He strives to attain the art that conceals art, thus insinuating himself into the confidence of the public. Honesty is not only the best policy but it is the only policy which makes possible the success of a persistent advertizing campaign.

The result of this combination of honesty and enterprize is that the American citizen and the American household are now buying an immense variety of things manufactured and distributed by the national advertizers, as they are called to distinguish them from the local merchants who can appeal only to the dwellers in their own more or less restricted areas. Probably very few of us have ever taken the trouble to count up the number of different articles daily delivered at our doors on order which are the direct or indirect result of advertizing. Even in staple articles of food, cereals, for example, we purchase package goods (warranted by the advertizer) in preference to the old-fashioned buying in bulk in which we had to rely on the integrity of the retailer. We do not now order a pound of oatmeal or of crackers; we specify the special brand which comes in a special container, and we thus assure ourselves as to quality and as to cleanliness.

IV

A century ago, not long after the end of the long Napoleonic wars, when Great Britain was staggering under a huge burden of debt, Sydney Smith wrote an article in which he set forth the unescapable incidence of taxation which every Englishman had to bear at every moment of his life from the cradle to the grave. It would be possible to paraphrase this famous passage and to show the American as subject now to advertizement as the Englishman then was to taxation. The American, after sleeping on an advertized mattress, gets out of an advertized bed and stands on an advertized carpet. In the bathroom he uses an advertized soap and an advertized tooth-paste. He puts on his advertized shoes and his advertized suit of clothes. His breakfast, prepared with the aid of an advertized kitchen-cabinet and an advertized stove, probably includes an advertized fruit, fresh or canned, an advertized cereal, and an advertized coffee. He takes his advertized hat and goes to his office, where he sits at his advertized desk. His letters are preserved in an advertized file, and his answers to them are printed on an advertized typewriter. And there is scarcely a moment of the day, from dawn to darkness, when he is not engaged in work or play, made possible or more convenient by the use of advertized devices of one sort or another.

It may be going a little too far to suggest that advertizing is one of the evidences of a high degree of civilization. Advertizing is a very modern art, perhaps the youngest of them; the Greeks knew it not, and the Latins were in little better case—altho they did scratch their *graffiti* on the walls of Pompeii. Even now the Chinese have not attained it, added testimony that their millennial culture is sadly backward. Perhaps there is even a hint of boastfulness in the suggestion that advertizing may serve as an index of culture when this suggestion is made by an American, since it is among us that the art flourishes most luxuriantly. But there is no vainglory in our pointing with pride to the fact that only on this side of the Atlantic could a bard find a sufficiency of resonant trademarks wherewith to build his ode, lofty in its aspiration even if it is likely to be less enduring than brass.

(1918.)

XI

A STANDARD OF SPOKEN ENGLISH

XI

A STANDARD OF SPOKEN ENGLISH

I

"WHAT is it that constitutes and makes man what he is?" Huxley asked in his discussion of 'Man's Place in Nature.' "What is it but his power of language—that language giving him the means of recording his experience, making every generation somewhat wiser than its predecessor, more in accordance with the established order of the universe?" Animals may have their simpler methods of conveying information and of communicating emotion, but man alone has developed the faculty of articulate speech which preceded and made possible the development of writing and of printing.

In these days when the printing-press is omnipresent, it seems to many to be omnipotent, and they are often inclined to consider the spoken word less useful and less important than the written. Yet this is a mistaken view, for speech not only came into being before writing, it is even now many times more abundant. Most of the business of life is still transacted by word of mouth. The telephone is daily gaining on its rivals, the telegraph and the post-office; and now the typewriter is becoming subservient to the dictaphone. Even in literature, altho history has long ceased to be an oral art akin to oratory, poetry does not come into its own until it is said or sung, making its ultimate appeal to the ear; and the drama is incomplete and comparatively inert until the give-and-take of its dialog is endowed with life by the voice of the actor.

"The spoken word is first in order and in dignity, since the written word is only its image, as the other is the image of the thought itself," so asserted Vaugelas, the regulator of usage in France nearly three centuries ago. And Socrates twenty centuries earlier had used the same figure, insisting that writing is the mere image or phantom of the living and animated word. The Greek philosopher asserted the abiding superiority of the spoken word over the written, since the latter—as Butcher summarized the objections—"has no power of adaptation; it speaks in one voice to all; it cannot answer questions, correct misunderstandings or supplement its own omissions." Here the inventor of the Socratic method is a little too emphatic, in so far at least as he may seem to suggest an inferiority of writing to speaking so complete as to render any record useless. Altho Socrates chose to express himself solely in speech, it is by the pages of Plato and Xenophon that his weighty utterances have been preserved for our profit.

There is no need now to dispute over the utility of the rival methods of human communication; each has its own opportunity. Writing is the more durable but speaking is the more individual, since we write for others, more often than not, whereas we speak rather for ourselves, in response to an uncontrollable need. Thus it is that there is likely to be a wider divergence in the speech of one man from that of another than there is in their respective writings. If a highlander of Scotland and a mountaineer of Georgia were to meet they would find in their several pronunciations and intonations a higher barrier to the interchange of information than they would discover if they were communicating with one another only by letter. The well-educated New Yorker and the well-educated Londoner when they take pen in hand are distinguishable by only a few localisms of vocabulary and usage; yet when they converse face to face their respective domiciles are likely to become instantly ascertainable.

In his illuminating discussion of the many misguided efforts of dictionary-makers to declare

an indisputable standard of English pronunciation, Lounsbury quoted Hawthorne as declaring that the pronunciation of *been* is an unfailing test of the nativity of a speaker, the Briton
riming it to *seen* and the American to *sin*.
Lounsbury also cited A. J. Ellis as preferring as
the test *trait*, which we on this side of the Atlantic
have frankly anglicized, riming it to *straight*,
whereas our kin across the sea have chosen to
preserve the original French sound, riming it
to *stray*. Lounsbury himself suggested that
schedule is better fitted to serve as a shibboleth
between the two greater divisions of the English-
speaking peoples, since it is almost the universal
custom of Americans to say *skedule* and of the
British to say *shedule*. Other observers might
readily find other words in which British usage
and American do not agree, altho there is not
the rigid uniformity on either side of the Western
Ocean that Hawthorne and Ellis asserted.

It has often been urged as an argument against
all effort to regularize our chaotic orthography
and to encourage our spelling to conform a little
less clumsily to our pronunciation, that any
attempt in this direction is but an idle dream,
since there is now no universally accepted pronunciation to which a simpler and more logical
orthography could adjust itself naturally. There
is no need to deny that this is a plausible objec-

tion; yet it will not withstand examination. True it is that there is nowhere to be found an inexpugnable authority having power to declare absolutely a final standard of pronunciation, and true it is also that there are many divergencies of utterance, national, sectional, local, and individual, yet this diversity is far less than might be supposed. A large part of it is unconscious and would be denied indignantly by a majority of those who are guilty of it. Men whose pronunciation may be slovenly to the very verge of illiteracy are often unaware of their linguistic delinquencies; and many of them would be greatly shocked if they could hear with their own ears an exact reproduction of their habitual utterances. The majority of us recognize that there is a normal pronunciation and we fondly believe that we conform to it. Indeed, when we speak in public, we generally make a strenuous effort to eliminate our personal peculiarities and to attain the standard that we accept.

II

Now if there is no authority to declare this standard, what is the normal pronunciation which we all, more or less, recognize and to which we seek to conform? How can there be any ideal uniformity of pronunciation between the British and the Americans? How could it exist in the United States when we can all of us distinguish at once the New Englander from the New Yorker, the man of the Middle West from the man of the Central South? And how could any such thing exist in Great Britain when everybody is aware of the very marked differences of speech between the Scotsman and the Yorkshireman, the Irishman and the Welshman, the cockney costermonger and the Oxford don? And then there are also the outlying possessions of the British Empire—there is Australia with its habits of speech modified by a climate very different from that which affects the utterances of the inhabitants of Canada. Yet we may find encouragement in the fact that the condition of English pronunciation is scarcely worse than that of French or German, Italian or Spanish.

Indeed, when we inquire more closely we discover that the situation in Spanish is not unlike that in English, since Spanish also is spoken by millions who no longer dwell in the land where the language came to its maturity; and yet the Spaniards have succeeded in establishing a standard of pronunciation and in adopting a spelling which is substantially fonetic. In one of his addresses as president of the Simplified

Spelling Board, Professor Grandgent reminded his hearers that "Spanish is, like English, a world-language, and its vast territory contains many varieties of current usage." Then he asked, "Upon what type is the spelling based? According to history, ancient tradition and present sentiment, the official speech of Spain and her offshoots is Castilian, and a sort of purified Castilian—more consistent and conservative than that which is now heard in the streets of Madrid—is the kind of Spanish represented by the common orthography, and regarded as a more or less remote ideal by the several Spanish provinces and nations. It must be confessed that in some of the countries of South America and even in Iberian Andalusia . . . the ideal is so remote as to be in danger of vanishing from the general consciousness. . . . But as long as the standard pronunciation is even vaguely present in the mind of a speaker, the orthography may, for that speaker, be called fonetic, tho his practise depart never so far from the ideal."

Just as Castilian is accepted as the standard of Spanish so Tuscan is accepted as the standard of Italian,—a language in which the orthography is also almost completely fonetic. No Italian child and no Spanish child is ever tortured by unremunerative toiling over a spelling-book.

213

Yet the divergencies of the local dialects in various parts of Italy from the Tuscan which is recognized as the ideal pronunciation are wider and more numerous than the corresponding divergencies in English. In the United States and in the British Commonwealth education is more widespread than in Italy or Spain or Spanish America; and wherever the schoolmaster is abroad there is an incessant pressure upon plastic youth to conform to the standard. Even if this conformity remains pitiably incomplete, at least there has been implanted a definite recognition of the existence of a norm and also an abiding respect for it.

As education is more thoro in France and in Germany than it is in Italy or in Spain, there has been a more striking success in imposing upon the French and the Germans a regard for the more or less remote ideal. In France, this ideal is found in the pronunciation of Paris,—altho there are those who are wont to contend for the superior purity of the speech of Tours. Of course, this ideal is not the casual and careless utterance of the average Parisian; it is that religiously conserved on the stage of the Théâtre Français. Years ago a highly cultivated teacher of French residing in New York told me that he felt it his duty to spend at least every other summer in assiduous attendance on the performances of the Comédie-Française that he might recover the felicities of accent for which his ear was likely to be blunted by too constant association with his American pupils, from whom he was in danger of acquiring perversities of pronunciation which demanded periodical eradication.

France has adopted as its standard an idealization of the speech of Paris, just as Spain has accepted an idealization of the speech of Madrid. But Germany has no capital; Berlin may assert itself, but Vienna and Dresden and Munich refuse to admit the supremacy of the Prussian metropolis; and a plea is often heard in behalf of Hanover as a city possessing a superior purity of speech—a plea akin to that advanced for Tours. In the long centuries when Germany was only a geographical expression, it could not possess a capital with the centralizing attraction of Paris and Madrid; and even after the creation of the German Empire, the other large cities were a little inclined to deride Berlin as an upstart, as an overgrown village, owing its unexpected expansion to a political accident.

The necessity for a standard of pronunciation was keenly felt in Germany, even if it could not be attained by the idealization of any local speech, and the problem of creating it was solved with Teutonic thoroness. The exciting cause of the action finally taken was the disastrous effect of local divergencies of pronunciation observable in the performances of the classics of the German drama, even when these were given by the carefully chosen and conscientiously trained companies of the court theaters. The Germans take the stage seriously, and the advantage of adopting a unified pronunciation for the use of actors was obvious to all lovers of the drama, who were continually in danger of having their attention distracted from the poetry of Schiller by jarring usages, often justified by irreconcilable traditions.

Professor Grandgent kindly supplied me with an account of the steps taken to establish a standard German for the stage. In 1896 Professor Theodor Siebs of Greifswald proposed the appointment of a commission to consist of actors, managers, and linguistic scholars, and his suggestion was approved in the following year by the General Superintendent of Royal Plays in Berlin, Graf von Hochberg, and by the German Philological Association. A committee of eleven was constituted in 1898, five professors representing the experts in language and six other members representing the actors and managers, chosen by the Deutscher Bühnenverein. Its sessions were held in the Apollo Hall of the Royal Theater in Berlin. The report was drawn

up by Professor Siebs; and its recommendations
were cordially received. As a result of this
application of the methods of scientific efficiency
to a linguistic difficulty there is now an authori-
tative *Bühnenaussprache,* a German equivalent
of the French pronunciation piously preserved
by the Comédie-Française.

III

"IT is universal suffrage which rules a language," so Sainte-Beuve reminded us; "and no
dictator has any authority." Yet a majority
of those interested may be quite willing to
abide by the decisions of a dictator-committee
composed of disinterested experts; and there
might be profit for us who have English for our
mother-tongue if we were to follow this German
example and to constitute an American-British
commission of actors and linguistic experts to
suggest a preference in all those cases where the
pronunciation is in dispute. It must be noted,
however, that the need for an artificially agreed
upon uniformity is not so obvious among the
English-speaking peoples as it was in the Ger-
man-speaking countries. For reasons partly
historical and partly literary we had a consciousness of a normal grammar, vocabulary,
and pronunciation centuries before this was

217

possible in a Germany which was for generations fragmentary, politically centrifugal, and
lacking the cohesive force of a vital literature.

Even now the condition of spoken English is
more satisfactory than that of spoken German,
in spite of the recent establishment of the
Deutsche Bühnenaussprache. It is true that
Dr. Robert Bridges, poet-laureate, has recently
held up his hands in horror at the vulgarian
atrocities, the distortions and dislocations recorded by the British phoneticians; and it is
true also that Henry James, in one of his flying
visits to his native land, was so profoundly
shocked by the slovenly utterances which fell
upon his refined ear that he "loosed the fateful
lightning of his wrath." Nevertheless the assertion may be ventured that no competent
observer could fail to find the speech of the
average Briton or American of fair education
less open to adverse criticism than the speech
of the average German of equivalent instruction.

To say this is not to deny that there are
dialectic and personal peculiarities audible both
in Great Britain and the United States. The
New Yorkers are as prompt to detect what we
call the "British accent" as the Londoners are
to recognize what they term the "Yankee
twang." Yet there are not a few speakers of
our tongue, born on one side of the Atlantic or

the other, who are almost altogether free from localisms of intonation and pronunciation. The tongue they speak is English at its best—not British and not American. I recall that I first noticed this a third of a century ago when I attended the dinner given in London to Henry Irving on the eve of his first visit to the United States, in 1883. Lord Coleridge presided, and Lowell made one of the happiest of his addresses —and while either of them was speaking the ears of the listeners were delighted by an English exquisite in its choice of words, and delicately harmonious in its intonations. What Lord Coleridge and Lowell spoke was English, pure and simple, not betraying itself as either British or American.

Of course, spoken English of this ultimate excellence is not common, any more than the spoken French of Coquelin, or the spoken German of Barnay; it could not but be rare, and therefore the more precious. Probably because my opportunities have been more frequent in the United States than in Great Britain, I should include more Americans than Britons on the list of those who have achieved it. I should enroll the name of President Eliot and not that of President McCosh. I should include John Hay and George William Curtis and not Matthew Arnold (who slighted his terminal *g's*) or Andrew Lang (whose early lowland Scotch was overlaid by later linguistic habits acquired in Oxford). I should leave off the name of Henry Irving as too individual and I should put on the name of Edwin Booth. I should exclude Clara Morris and Lawrence Barrett and I should include Agnes Booth and Herman Vezin. From among the more prominent performers on our stage to-day, it would be impossible not to inscribe upon the roll Ellen Terry, Ada Rehan and Julia Marlowe, Forbes-Robertson, John Drew, Otis Skinner and George Arliss. And I must beg to be excused from the invidious task of singling out certain other contemporary actors and actresses of Great Britain and the United States who fail conspicuously to attain to this international standard.

Fortunately the compassing of this lofty ideal is not strictly necessary in the presentation of the ordinary drama of the day dealing with a theme more or less local to one country or the other; it is not needed even when the original company transports the piece across the Atlantic. It is perhaps possible that an occasional spectator in London might feel that he had not got his money's worth if he failed to recognize the expected Yankee twang in one or more performers in an exclusively American cast of a characteristically American play; and in like manner the theatergoer of New York is quite as tolerant towards Briticisms of enunciation when he is beholding the representation of a British comedy by an exclusively British company as he is to the Briticisms of phrase which may besprinkle the dialog of the piece itself—locutions as unfamiliar to American ears as *Aren't I?* and *directly I arrived*. In fact, the localisms of phrase, like the corresponding localisms of pronunciation, might very well be defended by an ardent advocate of realism as helpful adjuncts to local color and as stricter approximations to the actual fact.

On the other hand American and British audiences are alike in desiring and even demanding a standardization of speech in the performance of plays of a larger import, wherein the actual fact yields to the essential truth. In any representation of the English classics, the tragedies of Shakspere or the comedies of Sheridan, and in any performance of translations of foreign masterpieces, the psychological fantasies of Maeterlinck or the social dramas of Ibsen, we expect uniformity of pronunciation and we are annoyed when our attention is distracted by inconsistencies in uttering *been* and *trait* and *schedule*, which reveal to us at once that the utterer is not a man of another time or another land but contemporaneously British or American.

It is therefore a good augury for the future to discover that so conscientious and so competent an observer as Professor Grandgent takes a very hopeful view of the outlook. "Dramatic tours, carrying actors from end to end of the English-speaking world, have made the approved practises of each great section familiar to every other part; while transference of performers from company to company and from country to country has worked for the establishment of an international theatrical standard. In the best performances of serious drama it is now often impossible for a spectator to tell whether a given actor is British or American." That is to say, these performers have succeeded in shedding whatever local peculiarities of pronunciation and of enunciation they may have originally possessed. No longer do they speak British-English or American-English; they speak English pure and simple, as did Lord Coleridge and Lowell. And this should be an ideal for all of us, whether native to the United States or to any part of the British Commonwealth.

(1916.)

XII

STYLE FROM SEVERAL ANGLES

XII

STYLE FROM SEVERAL ANGLES

I

WHEN we read the essays of Montaigne today, we do so in the latest of the four editions which he himself prepared for publication; and what we find therein is the frank and captivating disclosure of his own undulating and diverse personality. But if we go back to the first edition we are surprised to perceive that in this Montaigne talked very little about himself, content to comment casually on the passages from his favorite authors that he was quoting and juxtaposing. The recent investigations of scholarly French critics have made it plain that when Montaigne first sat down to write he felt little inclination to the self-analysis which is one of the chief attractions of his essays in their final form. His intention seems then to have been only to compile a modest commonplace book of extracts from the writers whom he had read long and often. In this first edition only now and again is he tempted to add anything personal to the quotations from the authors he relished. He was satisfied to supply only a ribbon of his own to bind together the garland he had woven of flowers plucked from many gardens. But as the years went by and as he added other transcriptions, annotating them and illuminating them with his own experiences and confessions, he began to take delight in chatting familiarly and in friendly fashion about himself. So it was that from edition to edition the book grew in bulk and burgeoned with his individuality, until at last that which had started with no desire for originality became one of the most original of books, not a mere mirror reflecting the angles of his library, but a hand-glass over the soul of Montaigne.

Montaigne's was a more leisurely age than ours, as Montaigne was more scholarly than most of those who today tread the trail he blazed. Yet there must be not a few men of letters nowadays who find time for varied reading, and who are tempted to copy out salient and significant sentences and to store them away against the hour of need, ready for use when occasion serves. As I have been trying for now more than fifty years to spy out a few of the secrets of the art of writing I have accumulated a lot of notable utterances on the fascinating subject of style. The hazard of a chance recovery of the envelop which had stood me in stead of the old-fashioned commonplace book has moved me to imitate—at a distance—the early manner of Montaigne and to weave a wreath of excerpts with only the necessary binding from my own stock. This is, perhaps, not quite so modest a task as it may seem, since I do not need to express my own opinions in my own words, as these will be evident enough from the words I have borrowed from others. A man cannot help making himself known by the quotations he has stored away.

What I have ever striven for as a writer is not a style of my own, not the acquiring of a distinctive and individual way of expressing myself, but the attainment of clarity. A precious compliment was paid to Macaulay when the proof-reader of his history told him that it had not been necessary to read any sentence twice to grasp its meaning. Of course, this compliment is also a criticism in its implication that Macaulay's thoughts were never so profound—or, if you please, so abstruse—as to demand concentrated effort for their apprehension. I could wish for the compliment; and I do not dread the criticism, as I have never had to deal with the profound or with the abstruse.

The first duty of the writer is to make the path easy for the reader, to grade the right of way so that the train of thought, heavy or light as the load may be, shall go on its course without annoying applications of the emergency brake. It is as true in this twentieth century as it was in the eighteenth, when Sheridan said it, that "easy writing is cursed hard reading." It is true also that style, in its masterly manifestations—the soaring eloquence of Burke, for example, and the severe elevation of Newman —is the lofty privilege of the gifted only; and those of us who are not gifted cannot achieve it by taking thought. But there are lowlier virtues which the humblest of us may attain.

Clarity, for example, does not vaunt itself, but its value is inestimable; and it is within the reach of the least endowed. In fact, it can be had for the asking, or at least it can be bought with a price. It may demand infinite care, protracted training, hard labor; what matter, if it is worth what it costs? When the British bard flattered Washington Irving by the assertion that the American author had "added clarity to the English language," he must, for the moment, have forgotten Bunyan and De Foe, Swift and Franklin, whose meaning is always unerringly apprehensible. Even if the poet was complimenting a new-comer in the field of letters at the expense of certain of his forerunners, he was none the less emphasizing the value of one of the most obvious qualities of Irving's work. Behind and beneath the charm and the grace of Thackeray's writing and of Howells' no less, there is an easy transparency by which their readers profit even if they fail to remark it.

The clarity of Irving and Thackeray and Howells is not so uncompromising as that of Macaulay. They do not argue with us; they only tell us, whereas Macaulay insists on driving home his points with repeated taps of the tack-hammer; and to avoid any possible confusion he does not shrink from the repetition of the essential words—a repetition which at times is almost tautology. Edward A. Freeman once asserted that Macaulay had taught him "never to be afraid of using the same word or name over and over again, if by that means anything could be added to clearness or force." Freeman declared that it was for others to judge whether he had learned from Macaulay the art of being clear, but he had at least learned from Macaulay "the duty of trying to be clear."

The difference between Macaulay and Freeman is that between a brilliant cavalry charge, "marshalled battalions bright in burnished steel," and the lumbering advance of a train of heavy artillery. It is a difference so wide that Freeman's style can scarcely be called a style; it is a stolid manner which fatigues far more

229

quickly than Macaulay's rapidity. Stevenson plainly goes too far when he calls Macaulay "an incomparable dauber," and when he suggests that it was probably for a "barbaric love of repeating the same sound rather than from any design of clearness" that Macaulay "acquired his irritating habit of repeating words." The artifice of Macaulay's antithesis and of his alliteration thrusts itself upon the reader's notice. Macaulay is not a dauber; he is an artist; but his brush-work is so bold that it obtrudes itself. He fails to conceal his art as well as he might. His is not "that exquisite something called style," which, so Lowell declared, "like the grace of perfect breeding, everywhere pervasive and nowhere emphatic, makes itself felt by the skill with which it effaces itself, and masters us at last with a sense of indefinable completeness."

II

HAS Dr. Johnson a style?—or is his manner of writing only a mannerism, not natural to him, and deliberately adopted? Certainly, it is everywhere emphatic and nowhere pervasive. Once upon a time when Canon Farrar had captured the unthinking with the protruded rhetoric of his 'Life of Christ,' a lady who was an enthu-

siastic admirer of his was taken in to dinner by
Dr. Thompson, the Master of Trinity. She
sang Canon Farrar's praises, and at last she
reached her climax: "and then, Master, Canon
Farrar has so much taste!" To which the ex-
asperated Dr. Thompson promptly retorted:
"He has indeed, madam, and all of it so bad!"
That the style of the great lexicographer was all
of it so bad, was also the opinion of a later dic-
tionary-maker, Noah Webster, who declared in
his 'Dissertations' that "the benefit derived
from his [Johnson's] morality and his erudition
will hardly counterbalance the mischief done
by his manner of writing."

Dr. Johnson's sesquipedalian ponderosity was
imposed on him by his mistaken understanding
of the demands of the dignity of literature. He
did not talk as he wrote—nobody ever did—and
this is the reason why he lives as a talker in
Boswell's pages while his own writings are now
read by title only. Yet unattractive as he is
in his works with their persistent and insistent
balance of polysyllabic noun with polysyllabic
noun, and of polysyllabic adjective with polysyllabic adjective, he is at least clear. We know
what he means and he makes us know it, even
if we are not interested. He parades his machinery, but the wheels do go round even if
they revolve slowly.

231

I remember my mother's telling me that in her school-days, now four score years ago, she had been taught that the opening sentence of 'Rasselas' was esteemed the most beautiful in the language. Here is that sentence:

Ye who listen with credulity to the whispers of fancy and pursue with eagerness the phantoms of hope, who expect that age will perform the promises of youth, and that the deficiencies of the present day will be supplied by the morrow, attend to the history of Rasselas, Prince of Abyssinia.

Recalling the hatred the author of 'Taxation no Tyranny' had for Americans, I feel that there is a certain piquancy in companioning this quotation from the most honored of British authors at the end of the eighteenth century with a quotation from an American author honored at the beginning of the twentieth century. After recording his pure bliss in the endeavor to transmute a German or Italian lyric into English verse, Howells went on to say that he sometimes thought there was "a finer pleasure in divining the subtle offices, the exquisite potentialities of prose. It is like walking in a fair country over a path that wanders at will among waving fields, beside rambling brooks, thru shadowy woods and sunny openings, all under a blue sky; and the birds flute and trill on every side; and when you will them the shy words come trooping, come flying, and settle in their chosen places as of their own accord, with no rhythmic compulsion and no metrical command. Prose, when it is perfected, will be as sweet as the talk of gracious-minded women, as simple and strong as the parlance of serious men; and it will not have to hide the art of its construction, for it will be a thing born, not made, and will live from the pen as it lives from the lips."

If the thought in the opening sentence of 'Rasselas' had occurred to Howells—and it is one of the eternal commonplaces which any essayist might find at the tip of his pen—with what delicate and delightful words would he have phrased it! And if Johnson had wanted to say what Howells has here uttered with his customary felicity, the burly Briton would have swathed it in cumbrous robes, whereby it would have lost its lightness and its ease, its grace and its charm. There would be no insuperable difficulty in turning Johnson's sentence into Macaulay or Howells' into Thackeray, but Howells' lovely phrases refuse absolutely to be translated into Johnsonese.

This impossibility is what Walter Bagehot made plain when he asserted that "if you will endeavor to write an imitation of the thoughts

233

of Swift in a copy of the style of Addison, you
will find that not only is it hard to write Addison's style from its intrinsic excellence, but also
that the more you approach to it the more you
lose the thought of Swift: the eager passion of
the meaning beats upon the mild drapery of
the words."

Probably no two writers who were contemporaries had styles more sharply dissimilar than
Cicero and Cæsar. Both of these Romans had
sat at the feet of the Greeks and had mastered
the complex technic of Attic rhetoric; both had
to deal with matters of state; and while Cicero
elaborated and decorated with unfailing certainty of effect, Cæsar wilfully achieved a stark
simplicity. Nobody has more aptly character-
ized Cicero's ornate method than Goumy, in
his posthumous essays on 'Les Latins': Cicero's
is "an enchanting prose, which shows no effort
nor tension nor shirking, as clear as the day, as
harmonious as music, flowing with the full
majesty of a great river, and as it flows rolling
all the riches of a superb language." On the
other hand Cæsar's 'Commentaries on the
Gallic War' has the stern concision of "a military report, sent back by a democratic general
to the people from whom he derived his powers,"
as Mommsen put it; and Cicero called it a work
of high value resembling "a beautiful antique

statue, as stripped of ornaments as that is of garments, and owing its beauty and its grace to its nudity."

No doubt, Cicero could have attained bare directness had he so desired and Cæsar could have been luxuriant; but each of them had an excellent reason for his choice. Cæsar was clear because he was simple and Cicero was clear even if he was not simple. Either of them would have betrayed himself if he had tried to employ the method of the other; and it would be as unprofitable to transmogrify Cæsar into Ciceronian or Cicero into Cæsarese as to transfer the thought of Swift into the style of Addison. After all, style is the man; and when it is not the fruit of his own spirit, it is illegitimate. It is then not good writing; it is only "fine writing." And fine writing is the abomination of desolation.

III

THE fine writers who insist on tying pink bows to all their thoughts fell under the displeasure of Sir Philip Sidney more than three centuries ago; he said they were like the Indians, because they were "not content to wear earrings at the fit and natural place of the ears, but they will thrust jewels through their noses and lips because they will be sure to be fine."

As I copy this out I am reminded of a kindred figure of speech to be found in an uncollected essay of Henry James', in which he says that Swinburne's style is "without measure, without discretion, without sense of what to take and what to leave; after a few pages, it becomes intolerably fatiguing," because "it is always listening to itself—always turning its head over its shoulders to see its train flowing behind it. The train shimmers and tumbles in a very gorgeous fashion, but the rustle of its embroidery is fatally importunate." And in another of his discarded criticisms he expressed his deep admiration for George Eliot's "perfect solid prose: brilliant and lax as it was in tissue it seemed to contain very few of the silken threads of poetry; it lay on the ground like a carpet, instead of floating in the air like a banner."

Here James' own style displays its silken threads and has the immitigable clarity which is ever the essential element of perfect solid prose, the very element which disappears in his later works, wherein we grope in a distilled darkness with never a thread, silken or hempen, to guide us out of the labyrinth. The early James seems to have been a fairly simple creature, whereas the later James was the most complicated of mortal men. Again style is the man himself. How can it ever be anything else and still be sincere? And the puzzle remains that a writer who had mastered modern French literature, who followed in the footsteps of Turgenief and who appreciated the sturdy vigor of Maupassant, an American who had lovingly but disinterestedly appreciated Hawthorne, could ever have been tempted to the raveling of hesitating convolutions. In his 'Recollections' Lord Morley records George Meredith's assertion that some pages in Charlotte Brontë's 'Villette' and some in Hawthorne's 'Marble Faun' are "the high-water mark of English prose in our time."

Hawthorne and Charlotte Brontë are a strange couple, and yet their respective styles have this in common, that they obey what Havelock Ellis has called "the law of the logic of thought." And the shrewd British critic declared that "all the conventional rules of the construction of speech may be put aside if a writer is thereby enabled to follow more closely the form and process of his thought. It is the law of that logic that he must forever follow, and in attaining it alone find rest. . . . The simple and naked beauty of Swift's style, sometimes so keen and poignant, rests absolutely on this truth to the logic of thought." And here we discover another reason why Swift cannot be translated into Addisonian.

It may be doubted whether Swift or Addison, Charlotte Brontë or Hawthorne ever worried their heads about style. They sought clarity and directness and simplicity. They seemed to have recognized that style is a little like happiness, in that it is likely to evade those who seek it too strenuously or too openly. Certainly they did not wrestle with the angel of the Lord as Carlyle did, panting with the fierce exertion. It would be amusing if we could have Swift's or Hawthorne's opinion of the hectic rhetoric of Ruskin and of the epicene fastidiousness of Pater.

Not only do the masters of style write with an apparently effortless ease, but they have often had to wait for the full recognition of their mastery. In reading the work of those who have clarity and directness, who match manner and matter, who obey the law of the logic of their thought, we are so satisfactorily carried along that at first we lack leisure to remark the sober artistry of their verbal craftsmanship. In their closely woven fabric there are no purple patches to take the eye and to demand instant acclamation. It was long years after John Bunyan was laid to rest that his command over our stubborn tongue began to receive the praise it deserved. And even now there are not so many as there might be who have discovered the unassuming Benjamin Franklin had a style of his own, as clear as Irving's or Addison's, easy and unobtrusive, and completely adequate to the expression of his common sense.

Probably Franklin and Bunyan would not quite know what to make of an often quoted passage in Stevenson's highly technical study of 'Style in Literature.' Often quoted this passage has been; and yet it must here be quoted once more if only to bring to a sonorous finish this medley of quotations: "We begin to see now what an intricate affair is any perfect passage; how many faculties, whether of taste or pure reason, must be held upon the stretch to make it; and why when it is made, it should afford us so complete a pleasure. From the arrangement of according letters, which is altogether arabesque and sensual, up to the architecture of the elegant and pregnant sentence, which is a vigorous act of the pure intellect, there is scarcely a faculty in man but has been exercised. He need not wonder, then, if perfect sentences are rare, and perfect pages rarer."

(1920.)

XIII

MARK TWAIN AND THE ART OF
WRITING

XIII

MARK TWAIN AND THE ART OF WRITING

I

IN an after-dinner speech which Mark Twain made in 1907 in London, at the Savage Club, he protested against an interviewer's having made him say that a certain address was *bully*, and he asserted that this distressed him, because "I never use slang to an interviewer or anybody else," adding that if he could not describe that address without using slang, he would not describe it at all. "I would close my mouth and keep it closed, much as it would discomfort me."

Possibly a few of those who heard Mark make this assertion, and probably more than a few of those who have read it in the volume in which his speeches are collected, may have been surprised and perhaps a little inclined to wonder whether Mark was not here indulging in his customary humorous unveracity. Some of them may have recalled the slang which fell unbroken from the lips of Scotty Briggs when he was enlisting the services of the preacher for Buck Fanshawe's funeral.

But in saying that he never used slang to an interviewer or anybody else, Mark was only asserting what must be plain to every careful reader of his works and to every one who has had the delight of hearing him tell a story. In the person of Scotty Briggs, who knew no other way of expressing himself, Mark could disclose his knowledge of the energetic and boldly imaginative speech of the unlettered Westerners:

> Phrases such as camps may teach,
> Saber-cuts of Saxon speech.

In his own person, as Samuel L. Clemens, or in his assumed personality, as Mark Twain, he refrained from this well of English undefiled by pernicketty precision, tempting as many of its vigorous vocables must have been to him, with his relish for verbal picturesqueness. He knew better than to yield to the easy allurement; and his English is as pure as it is direct and un-compromising. As he eschewed slang so he did not disfigure his pages with localisms, current only sectionally. He avoided dialectic peculi-arities however picturesque in themselves and however expressive. Of course he let his local characters express themselves in their local vernacular; and he took pride in the intimacy

244

of his acquaintance with sectional vagaries of vocabulary. In an explanatory note prefixed to 'Huckleberry Finn' he told his readers that he had therein used a number of dialects, "to wit: the Missouri negro dialect; the extremest form of the backwoods Southwestern dialect; and the ordinary Pike County dialect, and four modified varieties of this last. The shadings have not been done in a haphazard fashion, or by guesswork, but painstakingly, and with the trustworthy guidance and support of personal familiarity with all these several forms of speech." To a friend who had inquired as to his collaboration with Bret Harte in an unsuccessful and unpublished play, 'Ah Sin,' he explained that they had talked out the plot and that he had played billiards while his collaborator wrote the play, adding, "Of course, I had to go over it and get the dialect right. Bret never did know anything about dialect."

While Mark never conformed to the British standard, often insular, and sometimes parochial, he disclosed no individual aberrations either in vocabulary or in usage. The Americanisms he employed on occasion are all legitimate, in that they are what may be called American contributions to the language; and he enlisted very few even of these.

With his sensitiveness to the form and color

of words, he was acutely conscious of the many differences between our habitual speech and that of our kin across the sea. In a chapter, which was crowded out of 'A Tramp Abroad' to find refuge later in a volume of his sketches, he tells us of an interview he had with an Englishman who complimented him on his English. "I said I was obliged to him for his compliment —since I knew he meant it for one—but that I was not fairly entitled to it, for I did not speak English at all—I only spoke American." Then he pointed out that he judged that even the educated classes in England had once dropped their h's in *humble* and *heroic* and *historic*, "because your writers still keep up the fashion of putting *an* before those words, instead of *a*. This is what Mr. Darwin might call a rudimentary sign that an *an* was justifiable once and useful. . . . Correct writers of the American language do not put *an* before those words." And he concluded by assuring his chance companion that "if I wanted to, I could pile up differences here until I not only convinced you that English and American are separate languages, but that when I speak my native tongue in its utmost purity an Englishman can't understand it at all!"

This final statement is the extravagant whimsy of a humorist. Yet it is a fact that

Mark spoke his native tongue in its utmost purity, which is why every Englishman could understand him. He spoke pure English, as free from obtruded Americanisms as from obsolete Briticisms, the English current on both shores of "the salt, unplumbed estranging sea," the English of Defoe and Bunyan, of Franklin and Lincoln. He knew that English was his native tongue, a birthright and not a loan or a gift, and he was content with its ample resources, seeking always the exact noun and the inexorable adjective. As Howells put it with his delicate felicity, Mark "used English in all its alien derivations as if it were native to his own air, as if it had come up out of American, out of Missourian ground"; Howells also pointed out that Mark had a "single-minded use of words, which he employs as Grant did to express the plain, straight meaning their common acceptance has given them, with no regard to their structural significance or their philological implications. He writes English as if it were a primitive and not a derivative language, without Gothic or Latin or Greek behind it, or German or French beside it." And he added that the word Mark prefers is "the Abraham Lincolnian word, not the Charles Sumnerian; it is American, Western."

There is a superstition among those who have

been educated beyond their intelligence that no man can be a master of English who does not possess Latin, at least, and perhaps French also. But this absurdity is exploded by the vital vigor of Bunyan and Defoe, not less than by that of Franklin and Lincoln, Grant and Mark Twain. And the vitality of Mark's English was a gainer also by the fact that to him English was always a spoken tongue; he wrote as he talked; but then he was always as careful in his choice of words when he talked as when he wrote. He imparted to the printed page the vivacity of the spoken word, its swiftness and its apparently unpremeditated ease. His sentences never seem labored, no matter how deeply they may have been pondered. In reading them they appear spontaneous; and whatever the labor they may have cost him, they are not stained with the smoke of the casting or scratched with the mark of the file. Self-taught as he was, no apprentice to the craft of composition ever had a severer teacher. He so mastered the secrets of our stubborn tongue that he was able to write it as he spoke it, with precise accuracy and yet with flowing freedom.

In this Mark all unwittingly (for he was never interested in the history of critical theories) was only acting on the principle laid down two and a half centuries ago by Vaugelas, the linguistic law-giver of the French: "The rule is general and without exception, that what one does not say in speaking, one ought never to say in writing." And again: "The greatest of all errors in the matter of writing, is to think, as many do, that one must not write as one talks."

The same point had been made even earlier by the Italian Castiglione, in his own famous book on the 'Courtier': "Writing is nothing but a form of speaking, which continues to exist after man has spoken, and is, as it were, an image of the words he utters. It is consequently reasonable to use greater diligence with a view to making what we write more polished and correct, yet not to do this so that the written words shall differ from the spoken, but only so that the best in spoken use shall be selected for our composition."

This is precisely what Mark trained himself to accomplish. He selected for his composition the best in spoken use. He profited by one of the advantages of writing as we speak, if only we are in the habit of speaking with due respect for the nobility of our tongue, that he did not cumber his pages with dead and gone words. Like every growing language, English has a host of words which have fallen into innocuous desuetude, and are no longer under-

standed of the people. They might run off the
pen of the pedantic, but they never fell from
the lips of Mark Twain. He was a man of his
own time, with no hankering after the archaic.
His language is the living speech of those who
have English for their mother-tongue, however
scattered they may be on all the shores of all
the seven seas.

In his autobiography, from which only a few
passages were published in his lifetime, Mark
told us that when he made the overland trip
to Nevada (which he described in 'Roughing
It') he took with him Webster's Unabridged
Dictionary—an early testimony to his desire
to spy out the secrets of the mother-tongue.
It was a cumbrous impediment, and its carriage
was costly, since the stage-coach charged extra
baggage by the ounce. "And it wasn't a good
dictionary anyway—didn't have any modern
words in it, only had obsolete ones that they
used to use when Noah Webster was a child."

It must be noted also that Mark refrained
from the employment of the newest words, the
linguistic novelties which are on probation, as
it were, which may in time win acceptance but
which for the moment are only colloquialisms,
uncertain of their ultimate admission into the
vocabulary as desirable citizens.

II

IT was Mark's misfortune—in so far as it
long delayed his recognition as a writer to be
taken seriously—that he first won the favor
of the public, in the United States and also in
Great Britain, with the 'Innocents Abroad,' a
book of robust humor, mirth-provoking and
often rollicking in its extravagance. His readers thereafter looked into his successive volumes
for the fun they were in search of, and having
found it, abundant and sparkling, they sought
no further. If they had, they could not have
failed to find other things also, not humorous,
but grave and even pathetic. Yet even in the
'Innocents Abroad,' which compelled their
laughter, there are passages which ought to
have arrested the attention of those who do
not run as they read, passages which proved
that Mark was no mere clown, grinning through
a horse-collar, and applying mechanically the
formulas of John Phœnix and Artemus Ward.
There is, for example, the meditation before the
Sphinx:

The great face was so sad, so earnest, so longing, so
patient. There was a dignity not of earth in its mien,
and in its countenance a benignity such as never anything human wore. It was stone, but it seemed sen-

tient. If ever image of stone thought, it was thinking.
It was looking toward the verge of the landscape, yet
looking *at* nothing—nothing but distance and vacancy.
It was looking over and beyond everything of the present, and far into the past. It was gazing out over the
ocean of Time—over lines of century waves which, further and further receding, closed nearer and nearer together, and blended at last into one unbroken tide,
away toward the horizon of remote antiquity. It was
thinking of the wars of departed ages; of the empires it
had seen created and destroyed; of the nations whose
birth it had witnessed, whose progress it had watched,
whose annihilation it had noted; of the joy and sorrow,
life and death, the grandeur and decay, of five thousand slow revolving years. It was the type of an attri-
bute of man—a faculty of his heart and brain. It was
Memory—Retrospection—wrought into visible, tangible
form. All who know what pathos there is in days that
are accomplished and faces that have vanished—albeit
only a trifling score of years gone by—will have some
appreciation of the pathos that dwells in those grave
eyes that look so steadfastly back upon the things they
knew before. History was born—before Tradition had
being—things that were, and forms that moved, in a
vague era which even Poetry and Romance scarce
know of—and passed one by one away and left the
stony dreamer solitary in the midst of a strange new
age, and uncomprehended scenes.

This description of a work of man must be
companioned by the description of a work of
nature, contained in his second book of European
travel, 'A Tramp Abroad': It is a vision of
the Jungfrau, seen from Interlaken:

This was the mighty dome of the Jungfrau softly outlined against the sky and faintly silvered by the starlight. There was something subduing in that silent and solemn and awful presence; one seemed to meet the immutable, the indestructible, the eternal, face to face, and to feel the trivial and fleeting nature of his own existence the more sharply by the contrast. One had the sense of being under the brooding contemplation of a spirit, not an inert mass of rocks and ice,—a spirit which had looked down through the slow drift of the ages, upon a million vanished races of men, and judged them; and would judge a million more,—and still be there, watching, unchanged and unchangeable, after all life should be gone and the earth have become a vacant desolation.

In the writings of how many of the authors of the nineteenth century could the beauty and the power of these passages be equalled? Could they be surpassed in any of them?

The 'Innocents Abroad' was published in 1869, and 'A Tramp Abroad' in 1879; and in the course of the decade which intervened between these books Mark was called upon to speak at a dinner of the New England Society in New York. He chose as his topic the subject which forms the staple of our casual conversation, the weather. And never before had the demerits of the New England climate been delineated and denounced with such vigor and such veracity. Never before had Mark displayed more exuberantly the wealth of his whimsy.

And then at the very end he made a plea in extenuation for the misdeeds of the culprit he had held up to derision:

But, after all, there is at least one thing about that weather (or, if you please, effects produced by it) which we residents would not like to part with. If we hadn't our bewitching autumn foliage, we should still have to credit the weather with one feature which compensates for all its bullying vagaries—the ice-storm: when a leafless tree is clothed with ice from the bottom to the top—ice that is as bright and clear as crystal; when every bough and twig is strung with ice-beads, frozen dew-drops, and the whole tree sparkles cold and white, like the Shah of Persia's diamond plume. Then the wind waves her branches and the sun comes out and turns all those myriads of beads and drops to prisms that glow and burn and flash with all manner of colored fires, which change and change again with inconceivable rapidity from blue to red, from red to green, and green to gold—the tree becomes a spraying fountain, a very explosion of dazzling jewels; and it stands there the acme, the climax, the supremest possibility in art or nature, of bewildering, intoxicating, intolerable magnificence.

Only by quotation is it possible to indicate the sustaining dignity of Mark's thought, his interpreting imagination, the immeasurable range of his vocabulary, the delicate precision of his choice of words, and the certainty of his construction. To the three passages already

254

chosen for this purpose it is impossible not to append a fourth, taken from one of the last papers that he penned with his own hand, the account of the death of his youngest daughter, Jean, only four months before he was himself to die. It was written at intervals, after he was awakened on the morning before Christmas by the sudden announcement, "Miss Jean is dead!" and during the days that intervened until she was laid away by the side of her mother, her brother and her elder sister. He did not write it for publication; it was too intimate for that; but he told his future biographer that if it was thought worthy, it could appear as the final chapter in the autobiography, whenever that should at last be printed. In these broken paragraphs, set down from hour to hour while he was stunned by the blow, he attained to the severest simplicity, the sincere simplicity of the deepest feeling. The selections must be few and brief:

Jean lies yonder,—I sit here; we are strangers under our own roof; we kissed hands good-by at this door last night—and it was forever, we never suspecting it. She lies there, and I sit here—writing, busying myself, to keep my heart from breaking. How dazzling the sunshine is flooding the hills around! It is like a mockery.

Seventy-four years and twenty-four days ago. Seventy-four years old yesterday. Who can estimate my age to-day?

.   .   .   .

Would I bring her back to life if I could do it? I would not. If a word would do it, I would beg for strength to withhold the word. And I would have the strength; I am sure of it. In her loss I am almost bankrupt, and my life is a bitterness, but I am content: for she has been enriched with the most precious of all gifts—that gift which makes all other gifts mean and poor—death.

III

It is a strange fact that few of those who have written about Mark Twain have called attention to his mastery of style, and that even fewer have paid attention to the essays and the letters in which he himself discussed the art of writing. Perhaps this is just as well, since his own work has been judged free from any bias aroused by his criticism of other men's writing. It may have been a disadvantage to Howells and Henry James and Robert Louis Stevenson that they approved themselves as critics as well as novelists, and that they were frank in expressing their opinions and in formulating their theories about the art of fiction and the art of writing; and it may be that the reticence in regard to these matters observed by Hawthorne and Hardy and Kipling is wiser. Mark's ventures into criticism are not many, but they are significant, and they shed light upon his own artistic standards.

There is illumination, for example, in one of the maxims of Pudd'nhead Wilson's Calendar: "As to the Adjective: when in doubt, strike it out." It would be useful to have that stamped in gold on the border of the blotting-pad of many a man of letters. And there are other remarks equally suggestive, scattered through his letters and through his essays on Howells as a master of English, on 'Fenimore Cooper's Literary Offences,' and 'In Defence of Harriet Shelley.'

The predisposing condition which led Mark to take up his pen in defence of Shelley's wife was his manly detestation of insinuating insincerity, and the exciting cause was his perusal of Dowden's unfortunate biography of her husband. Mark was moved to wrath, as well he might be, by Dowden's special pleading, by his maneuvers to whiten Shelley by blackening Shelley's wife. Mark begins by a characterization of Dowden's style:

Our negroes in America have several ways of entertaining themselves which are not found among the whites anywhere. Among these inventions is one which is particularly popular with them. It is a competition in elegant deportment. . . . Cake is pro-

vided as a prize for the winner in the competition. . . .
One at a time the contestants enter, clothed regard-
less of expense in what each considers the perfection
of style and taste, and walk down the vacant central
space and back again . . . all that the competitor
knows of fine airs and graces he throws into his carriage, all that he knows of seductive expression he
throws into his countenance. . . . They call it a
Cake-Walk. The Shelley biography is a literary cake-
walk. The ordinary forms of speech are absent from
it. All the pages, all the paragraphs walk by sedately,
elegantly, not to say mincingly, in their Sunday best,
shiny and sleek, perfumed, and with *boutonnières* in their
button-holes; it is rare to find even a chance sentence
that has forgotten to dress.

From this expressive characterization it is
plain that Dowden had a liking for what Kipling has described as "the Bouverie-Byzantine
style, with baroque and rococo embellishments";
and that Mark Twain did not share this liking.
He detested humbug and pretense and preten-
tiousness. Affectation in all its myriad aspects
was ever abhorrent to him; and what he most
relished in an author was a straightforward
concreteness of presentation. We may be sure
that he would have approved Brunetière's assertion that "a good writer is simply one who says
all he means to say, who says only what he
means to say, and who says it exactly as he
meant to say it."

It was the false tone and the unfair intent of

Dowden's book which compelled Mark to his merciless exposure. In his less carefully controlled essay on 'Fenimore Cooper's Literary Offences,' he impaled the author of the 'Leather Stocking Tales' for the verbal inaccuracies not infrequent in Cooper's pages. Mark declared that the rules for good writing require that "an author shall say what he is proposing to say, not merely come near it; use the right word, not its second cousin; eschew surplusage; not omit necessary details; avoid slovenliness of form; use good grammar; and employ a simple and straightforward style." He insisted that all seven of these rules, of these precepts for correct composition, "are coldly and persistently violated in the 'Deerslayer' tale."

A little later in his searching criticism Mark becomes more specific. He tells us that "Cooper's word-sense was singularly dull. When a person has a poor ear for music he will flat and sharp right along without knowing it. He keeps near the tune, but it is *not* the tune. When a person has a poor ear for words, the result is a literary flatting and sharping; you perceive what he is intending to say, but you also perceive that he doesn't *say* it. This is Cooper. He was not a word-musician. His ear was satisfied with the *approximate* word." Even an ardent admirer of the broad bold pictures of life in the green forest and on the blue water painted in the 'Last of the Mohicans' and in the 'Pilot' cannot but admit that there is not a little justice in Mark's disparaging criticism. Cooper is not a word-musician; he sometimes flats and sharps; and he is often content when he has happened on the approximate term. But the seven rules here cited, while they cast light on Cooper's deficiencies also illuminate Mark's own standards of style. He was annoyed by Cooper's occasional carelessness in the use of words, as many other readers must have been; but Mark was more annoyed than most of these other readers because his own practise had made him inexorable in precision. He himself was never satisfied with the approximate word; he never flatted or sharped; he had a word-sense that was always both acute and alert.

Altho he never prepared a paper on Walter Scott's literary offences, Mark held that the author of 'Guy Mannering' had been guilty of verbal misdemeanors as heinous as those of the author of the 'Last of the Mohicans.' And in a letter that he wrote to me in 1903 he asked a series of questions which he obviously held to be unanswerable:

Are there in Sir Walter's novels passages done in good English—English which is neither slovenly nor involved? Are there passages whose English is not poor and thin and commonplace, but is of a quality above that? Did he know how to write English, and didn't do it because he didn't want to? Did he use the right word only when he couldn't think of another one, or did he run so much to wrong because he didn't know the right one when he saw it?

Here again the loyal lover of 'Quentin Durward' and of the 'Heart of Midlothian' cannot deny that there are inaccuracies and inelegancies in Scott's flowing pages, and quite enough of them, to make it a little difficult to enter a general denial of all these piercing queries. Scott did not take his fiction over-seriously. He was, as Carlyle put it bluntly, "improvising novels to buy farms with." His style, like his construction, is sometimes careless, not to call it reckless. Mark had trained himself to be careful and to take delight in the dexterities of verbal adjustment; and this had made him intolerant of the verbal untidiness, so to term it, perhaps not so frequent in Scott as in Cooper, but far too frequent in both of them, even if their works had major merits which Mark was led to overlook in his disgust at their minor lapses from literary propriety.

Besides calling attention to these linguistic defects, Mark took occasion also in the essay on Cooper and in a letter on Scott to express his dislike for their stories, merely as stories. He held that Cooper violated the rules which require that "a tale shall accomplish something and arrive somewhere"; that "the episodes of a tale shall be necessary parts of the tale, and shall help to develop it"; that "the personages in a tale shall be alive, except in the case of corpses, and that always the reader shall be able to tell the corpses from the others"; and that "the personages in a tale, both dead and alive, shall exhibit a sufficient excuse for being there." He asked whether Scott has "personages whose acts and talk correspond with their characters as described by him"? Whether he has "heroes and heroines whom the reader admires, admires and knows *why*"? Whether he has "funny characters that are funny, and humorous passages that are humorous"? And he asserted that "it is impossible to feel an interest in these bloodless shams, these milk-and-water humbugs. And oh, the poverty of the invention! Not poverty in inventing situations, but poverty in furnishing reasons for them."

Here we come face to face with one of Mark's most obvious limitations as a critic of literature: he is implacable in applying the standards of today to the fiction of yesterday. Despite their occasional slovenliness of diction and their constant heaping up of adventure upon adventure, Scott and Cooper could create accusable

characters, standing upright on their own feet
and dominating the situations in which they
are immeshed. But each of these bold story-
tellers did this in his own fashion, in the fashion
of his own time, for they knew no other, and
they could not foresee that their methods would
be demoded in five score years. Howells was
right when he declared that the art of fiction
is a finer art now than it was only half a century ago. Of course it is; and so is the art of
the drama and the art of painting also. And
equally of course this declaration carries with
it no implication that the artists of the present
are mightier than the masters of the past.
There were giants in those days, as we all know,
but these giants were not armed and equipt
with the weapons of precision now available for
men of only ordinary stature. The state of
an art—whichever this art may be, fiction or
drama or painting—is never stationary; and its
processes are continually modified and multiplied.

One explanation for Mark's error of judgment is probably that he is a realist, with all
the realist's abiding abhorrence for romanticism,
wilful, arbitrary and highflown, for its striving
after vivid external effects, and for the departure
from veracity which this seeking entails. He
so detested the attitude of Scott and Cooper,

he was so painfully annoyed by their frequent failure to pierce below the surface of life that he blinded himself to their major merits, to the outstanding qualities which make them majestic figures in the history of fiction, however old-fashioned their way of telling a story and however blundering their use of language. But this explanation will not serve to elucidate the reason for his hatred of Jane Austen's novels. She was also a realist and a humorist, and her style is not open to the strictures which Scott and Cooper invite by their haste in composition. Yet he once wrote to a friend that he had often wanted to criticize Jane Austen, "but her books madden me so that I can't conceal my frenzy from the reader; and therefore, I have to stop every time I begin. Every time I read 'Pride and Prejudice' I want to dig her up and beat her over the skull with her own shin-bone!"

There is no denying the vernacular vigor of this whimsical ebullition. Mark knew well enough what he did not like; but why didn't he like Jane Austen? And the answer is far to seek. Perhaps it is that Jane Austen is a miniaturist of exquisite discretion, not a mural painter, because she molds a Tanagra figurine and not the Winged Victory, because her little miracles of delicate observation seemed to him only the

264

carving of cherry-stones. Her field is limited and her vision, keen as it is, is restricted; whereas Mark was wont to survey the full spectroscope of American life—that spectroscope which may seem at times to be almost a kaleidoscope. It may be, however, that the explanation lies a little deeper, in the difference between the clever spinster of Winchester and the robust humorist of Hannibal, Missouri. It may be that with Mark's ingrained democracy he was outraged by Jane's placid and complacent acceptance of a semi-feudal social organization, stratified like a chocolate layer-cake, with petty human fossils in its lower formations.

IV

It is only fair to note that Mark never did write a criticism of Jane Austen, altho he once went out of his way (in 'Following the Equator') to speak disparagingly. He expressed his desire to desecrate her grave only in a letter to an intimate familiar with his imaginative exaggeration. In the same letter he confessed that he had no right to criticize books, because he could not keep his temper. "I don't do it, except when I hate them." He hated Dowden's biography of Shelley and for good reason, since it is intellectually dishonest. He persuaded

265

himself that he hated Cooper's 'Deerslayer';
and admirers of the 'Leather Stocking Tales'
must admit that he had a case, even if he does
not win a verdict from the jury.

Once, and once only, was he moved to criticism, not by hate but by love, by a sincere
appreciation of the superb craftsmanship of a
fellow-practitioner of the art of fiction. His
unbroken friendship with Howells is one of the
most salient in all the long history of literature,
worthy to be set by the side of those of Molière
and Boileau, Goethe and Schiller, Emerson and
Carlyle. It endured cloudless for two score
years; and its full significance will not appear
until the letters they interchanged are collected
and published. Four years before he died
Mark wrote a brief essay on Howells. It is a
study of style, of Howells' command over the
language, of the characteristics which combine
to make Howells one of the indisputable masters of our stubborn speech:

For forty years his English has been to me a con-
tinual delight and astonishment. In the sustained exhibition of certain great qualities—clearness, compres-
sion, verbal exactness, and unforced and seemingly unconscious felicity of phrasing—he is, in my belief, without his peer in the English-writing world. . . . There
are others who exhibit these great qualities as greatly
as does he, but only by intervalled distributions of rich

moonlight, with stretches of veiled and dimmer landscape between; whereas Howells' moon sails cloudless skies all night and all the nights.

Mark found in Howells' writing the very virtue which he failed to find in Cooper's (who worked, it must again be pointed out, more than four score years earlier):

In the matter of verbal exactness, Mr. Howells has no superior, I suppose. He seems to be almost always able to find that elusive and shifty grain of gold, the *right word*. Others have to put up with approximations more or less frequently; he has better luck. To me, the others are miners working with the gold-pan—of necessity some of the gold washes over and escapes; whereas, in my fancy, he is quicksilver raiding down a riffle—no grain of the metal stands much chance of eluding him.

And then Mark gives us an explanation of the ultimate value of the right word—an explanation certain to be quoted again and again in our future manuals of composition:

A powerful agent is the right word; it lights the reader's way and makes it plain; a close approximation to it will answer, and much travelling is done in a well-enough fashion by its help, but we do not welcome it and applaud it and rejoice in it as we do when *the* right one blazes out on us. Whenever we come upon one of those intensely right words in a book or a newspaper the resulting effect is physical as well as spiritual, and electrically prompt: it tingles exquisitely around through the walls of the mouth and tastes as tart and crisp and good as the autumn-butter that creams the sumac-berry.

These quotations reveal Mark's own standards of style as sharply as they illuminate Howells' practise. And yet another quotation, the last of all, imposes itself, because it exemplifies Mark's own mercurial clutch on the right word:

As concerns his humor, I will not try to say anything, yet I would try if I had the words that might approximately reach up to its high place. I do not think any one else can play with humorous fancies so gracefully and delicately and deliciously as he does, nor has so many to play with, nor can come so near making them look as if they were doing the playing themselves and he was not aware they were at it. For they are unobtrusive and quiet in their ways, and well conducted. His is a humor which flows softly all around about and over and through the mesh of the page, pervasive, refreshing, health-giving, and makes no more show and no more noise than does the circulation of the blood.

Did any humorist ever praise another with a more absolute understanding and with a more certain insight into the essence of the most delicate humor?

(1920.)

XIV

ONE WORLD–LANGUAGE OR TWO?

XIV

ONE WORLD–LANGUAGE OR TWO?

I

MORE than a score of nations were at war with the German Empire and its vassal states; and the alliance between the various and disparate countries banded together in defense of civilization grew closer as they severally discovered the absolute necessity of unity of purpose. It was proved that they could act together in war-time; and, therefore, the question is being raised on all sides whether they cannot retain a friendly understanding now that peace has been won. The advantages of their association to repel the ruthless aggressor have been so obvious that there is a strong desire to preserve these advantages when the military struggle shall be succeeded by an economic rivalry likely to be almost as fierce.

Whether the alliance continues in some loose form or not, the parties to it have come to know one another better than they ever did before; and they have come to feel the need of a more sympathetic international understanding. It is not surprising, therefore, that a cry has arisen on both sides of the Atlantic for the adoption of a universal language by means of which the peoples of all the scattered allied states could communicate freely and spontaneously. If the inhabitants of France and Italy, of Rumania and Portugal, of the British Commonwealth and the United States are to be knit together by a more intimate friendliness, they would profit by the possession of a common speech in which to hold converse with one another.

This has led enthusiasts in London and in New York to urge that steps be taken at once to adopt as a universal speech either one of the existing racial tongues or one of the artificial languages of which half-a-dozen have been made to order in the past half-century. One American advocate of immediate action asserted that "the need is here and now—real, positive, pressing"; and he was insistent that the allied governments in conjunction with the few neutral powers should "select some one existing language, to be made a part of the regular tuition in the schools of all countries—side by side, of course, with the existing language of each country." He quoted aptly from Charles Reade's the 'Cloister and the Hearth'—"For what are all your barbarous jargons but barriers between men's hearts?"

272

This American correspondent concluded by
expressing his natural belief that the chosen
language should be English. But at almost the
same time that his appeal appeared in a New
York newspaper, a British correspondent of a
London newspaper, admitting the necessity of
adopting an existing language as a medium for
international communication, opposed the choice
of any racial tongue as likely to arouse national
rivalry, and suggested that if the living languages had to be excluded from the selection,
it would be well to revive one of the dead languages; and he gave his own vote for Latin.
At first sight, this would seem to be an impossible proposal, and yet on examination it is discovered to have a certain plausibility.

We all know that for a thousand years and
more Latin was employed as a world-language.
It was the one tongue familiar to all men of
education. Thruout the far-flung battle-line
of the Roman Empire, it served in the forum,
in the market-place, and on the tented field.
The Romans might admire the nobility and the
flexibility of Greek, and they might even admit
its superiority over Latin, but they insisted
on conducting the business of their empire in
their own tongue. Gibbon tells us that the
Emperor Claudius "disfranchised an eminent
Grecian for not understanding Latin"; and the

Roman speech long survived the decline and fall of the Roman Empire. Latin lingered as the sole medium for the intercommunication of scholars until long after the Renascence had spent its force. Dante and Bacon and Milton wrote in Latin, even if their fame rests wholly upon their works in their native idioms.

We must also remember that, altho Latin is often carelessly classed as a dead language, it is still a living tongue in the Catholic Church. The liturgy of this church is read and sung in Latin; the Pope's state-papers are written in Latin; and in many of the Jesuit colleges a large part of the instruction is in Latin. The language has been kept alive for the use of theology and of philosophy, and even of literature. But its vocabulary would be found painfully inadequate even to name a host of modern things that the Romans could not foresee. To be of use in the finance, the manufacturing, and the commerce of tomorrow, Latin would need to be expanded immeasurably; and even then the result would not be wholly satisfactory. A large body of the most learned literary experts might toil long and laboriously before they could devise Latin equivalents for the specific terms of the electrician and the biologist, the devotee of golf and of baseball, the art-critic and the dressmaker.

II

IF no dead tongue can be recalled to life and galvanized into impossible activity, we must adopt one of the living languages and impose the study of this upon the citizens of all the lands where it is not already the native speech, or we must fall back on one of the artificial tongues. The American correspondent, from whom quotation has already been made, ruled out German, of course, as a barbarous jargon; it is the most uncouth, the most awkward, the least advanced of all the modern tongues; and it is therefore the least fit to be a medium of international communication—even if there were not other and more obvious reasons for refusing to consider it. The choice would lie between French and English, of course.

English is now the native speech of the inhabitants of a very large part of the earth's surface, and its expansion in the nineteenth century is one of the most striking phenomena of that phenomenal epoch. French is still the language of diplomacy; it is still the second language most likely to be acquired by the educated men of all countries. The literatures of the two languages have grown side by side for nearly a thousand years, until each of them is richer than the literature of any other tongue, even if those other tongues have been made illustrious by sporadic men of genius. Each has its merits and its weaknesses; but each is fit for service thruout the world. There would be immense advantage if one or the other could be imposed on the peoples who do not possess it.

But this advantage will never accrue to the human race by international agreement. An adoption by joint action of either English or French is beyond the range of the possible; it is an iridescent dream. It is inconceivable that the inhabitants of the British Isles, of the scattered dominions which are proud to be included in the British Commonwealth, and of the United States, should ever agree to impose upon all its youth the acquisition of French. And it is equally impossible that the Latin races, the French, Belgians and Swiss, the Spanish-speaking peoples, the Portuguese and the Rumanians, should require their children to master a Teutonic tongue entirely foreign to their speech habits.

And this would seem to leave the field open for an artificial tongue, Volapük, Esperanto, or Ido, each of which has or has had its enthusiastic advocates. Volapük may be disregarded, as it was cumbered with grammatical complexities long since discarded in English; and the vogue of Esperanto was waning even before the World

War. But Ido is far less unsatisfactory than its two predecessors; it is euphonious, flexible, and easy to learn. One of its American admirers has asserted that it comes very near to perfection, and that its lack of patriotic associations will be no bar to its utility for international purposes. Possibly its undeniable merits may win for Ido the approval of those who are so unfamiliar with the history and the growth of language as to believe in the permanent utility of a speech deliberately manufactured.

One of the most obvious advantages of a living speech is that whenever a new thing comes into existence, needing an immediate name, this name is instantly supplied by one of those who is using the new thing. Every living language is developing spontaneously, and without control; and the various crafts and professions are forever enlarging their vocabularies. Now an international language must renounce spontaneity and the free creation of new words; it must submit to some central authority which will impose the obligatory international uniformity. But even if this insuperable difficulty could be overcome, any artificial language would be under another disadvantage as a medium for international communication. In conversation or correspondence between two persons of different nationality, the artificial language would not be the native speech of either party. They would both of them be grappling with the difficulties of an idiom which was not their own.

There is, however, a third reason why no artificial language will ever be imposed on school children by the common consent of the civilized nations, or will ever be able to spread itself widely without governmental compulsion. This final reason is simply that the sturdy common sense of mankind will forever refuse to undergo the long labor of acquiring a language without a literature, and without a historic past, a language to be spoken only by those willing to take the trouble to master it, a language which is not the native speech of millions of people, making it in their own image and impressing upon it their racial characteristics.

III

If then there is no likelihood that an association of friendly allies will formally adopt any one language, living or dead or still-born (as all the artificial tongues must be), and impose its acquisition upon all the children, are we therefore to be deprived of all the obvious advantages of a world-language? Are we to continue to dwell unresisting in the shadow of the Tower of

Babel? Must we suffer forever from the evil consequence of the Confusion of Tongues? Well, if we are discouraged by the fact that international action is impossible, we may find encouragement in the facts which go to show that international action may not be as necessary as its advocates have asserted. In other words, perfectly natural causes may be at work now to ameliorate our existing linguistic chaos.

In a lecture before the armistice on 'Some Gains of the War,' Professor Walter Raleigh asserted that "after the war the English language will have such a position as it never had before; it will be established in world-wide security." No doubt, the position of English is now more secure; but there was no danger to its security before the invasion of Belgium. It was the native tongue of more than a hundred and fifty millions of men, women and children; and it was the official language of many millions more in India, in Egypt, and in the Philippines. It was spreading more rapidly than any other idiom.

Professor Raleigh was eloquent in praise of our sturdy language; and he did not feel called upon to say anything in behalf of French. But it is obvious enough that the French language is also established in world-wide security. The French are the foremost of the Latin peoples,

279

and the other Latin peoples accept their leadership.

There is no probability that any international action will impose the study of English upon the Latin peoples, or the study of French upon the Teutonic peoples; but there is every probability that the supremacy of French among the Latin tongues and the supremacy of English among the Teutonic tongues will be more and more widely recognized, so that the voluntary acquisition of one or the other of these supreme languages will become more and more customary among the peoples to whom neither tongue is native. It is certain, moreover, that the prolonged stay of millions of English-speaking soldiers in France will increase the number of the French who speak English and of the Americans, the Australians, the Canadians, and the English who speak French. There will be an accelerated desire on the part of the soldiers of every nation to become bilingual.

This tendency will be fostered by the closer friendships created between the allies by the war. There will be no need of an international agreement to compel the educational authorities of the United States and of the British Commonwealth to foster the study of French—the more especially as French will be freed from the former rivalry of German. And in like manner the educational authorities of France and of Belgium are certain to encourage in every way the study of English. The inevitable result will be that we shall have made an unexpected approach to the international world-language which is so greatly to be desired. We shall not have a single world-language, but we shall have two world-languages, friendly rivals, and dreading no rivalry with any other tongue. The competition of German is no longer to be feared, as it will be an abhorred idiom for many years to come, and we may even venture to suggest that in the immediate future the students of Spanish will far outnumber the students of German, and the Germans themselves will be forced to continue their useful habit of acquiring both French and English.

(1919.)

BIBLIOGRAPHIC NOTE

Other papers by the same writer on kindred topics will be found in other volumes.

In 'Pen and Ink: Essays on Subjects of More or Less Importance' (1888) there is a paper

'On the French Which is Spoken by Those Who Do Not Speak French.'

In 'Parts of Speech: Essays on English' (1901) there are papers entitled

'The Stock That Speaks the Language.'
'The Future of the Language.'
'The English Language in the United States.'
'The English Language in Great Britain.'
'Americanisms Once More.'
'New Words and Old.'
'The Naturalization of Foreign Words.'
'The Function of Slang.'
'Questions of Usage.'
'An Inquiry as to Rime.'
'On the Poetry of Place Names.'
'As to American Spelling.'
'The Simplification of English Spelling.'
'Americanism: An Attempt at a Definition.'

In the 'American of the Future' (1909) there are papers entitled

'The Speech of the People.'
'English as a World-Language.'
'Simplified Spelling and Fonetik Reform.'

In the 'Principles of Playmaking, and Other Discussions of the Drama' (1919) there is a paper on

283

BIBLIOGRAPHIC NOTE

'The Vocabulary of the Show-Business.'
Also to be recorded are two pamphlets entitled the
'Spelling of Yesterday and the Spelling of Tomorrow'
(1906), and the 'Spelling of the Poets' (1908), issued
by the Simplified Spelling Board; and a third, entitled
the 'Englishing of French Words' (1921), issued by the
Society for Pure English.

S